# Everything You Know About Investing Is Wrong

# Everything You Know About Investing Is Wrong

JOHN K. SOSNOWY WITH KORI S. VOORHEES

Neither the authors nor the publisher is engaged in rendering financial, legal, or accounting services to the reader through the sale of this book. The opinions and information rendered herein are those of the authors as individuals and do not represent the official position of any firm with whom they are affiliated. Since individual situations do vary, the reader should consult a competent professional on questions specific to the individual. The authors and the publisher disclaim any liability for any loss incurred, directly or indirectly, as a consequence of the use or application of any information contained in this book.

This book was printed in the United States of America.

**To order additional copies of this book, contact:**
Xlibris Corporation
1-888-795-4274
www.Xlibris.com
Orders@Xlibris.com
18098-VOOR

## Advance Praise for
*Everything You Know About Investing Is Wrong*

"I have read hundreds of books on investing. This one ranks at the top of the list. No one has more insights into the value of active management than John. If you read only one book on investing, this is the one!"

Roger Schreiner, Founder and President
Schreiner Capital Management, Inc. and
The Select Advisors Program

"Congratulations on another book well done. I considered your first book a very important read for investors but I think this book should be required reading for investors of all experience levels before they make their next investment. You have successfully delivered the message of how every investor can attain long-term profitability with peace of mind."

Peter Mauthe, Chief Operating Officer
Spectrum Financial, Inc.

"I think you did an outstanding job on this (book). I wish I would have written it, but (I) probably (would) not (have written it) as well as you did."

Joseph Ludwig, President
Tandem Financial Services, Inc.

"It is a great and timely book . . . . Jonathan Swift said, 'Truths languish, while myths flourish.' Nowhere does such flourishing take place more than in investing. Every *objective* investor would be well served indeed by reading this myth buster."

John Lyons, President
J. Lyons Fund Management

"Turning conventional wisdom on its ear, John Sosnowy's follow-up to *Lasting Wealth Is A Matter Of Timing* proves, once again, that eating well and sleeping well are NOT mutually incompatible goals—a must read."
Hays Glover, President
Warwick Investment Management, Inc.

"401(k) plans, IRA rollovers, retirement savings . . . never before has the responsibility for investing been thrust on so many individual investors, the vast majority of whom lack the investment education and the necessary time to properly monitor and manage their investments. Millions of novice investors have entered the Wall Street arena—an arena where minnows get eaten by sharks. John's book exposes the Buy and Hold investment myths and gives the reader a clear, understandable path toward a vastly more prudent Active Risk Management investment approach."
Steve Blumenthal, President and CEO
Capital Management Group, Inc. and President, SAAFTI

"In his new book, *Everything You Know About Investing Is Wrong*, author Sosnowy demonstrates that he is neither fooled nor intimidated by the shibboleths of the entrenched financial-planning establishment. I recommend this book for the investor who is prepared to critically examine some commonly-held (but wrong) beliefs and chart his own course."
Steve Shellans, Editor
MoniResearch Newsletter

"Your approach of focusing on key Myths that the consuming public has about investing brings concepts that are sometimes complex to an understandable level, thus making your recommendations more likely to be acted on by the consuming public. And given the likely position of their investment portfolio today, action does need to be taken—action such as the active risk management outlined in your book."

Steve Gradeless, National Sales Manager
America's MarketFlex Annuity
Nationwide Financial Services

"Finally, someone has exposed the conventional wisdom of Wall Street for what it really is—ill-conceived mythology, with little connection to the realities of today's markets. John's book is essential reading for real world investors!"

Jerry Wagner, Chairman and CEO
Flexible Plan Investments, Ltd.

To Colby and Kori:
Thanks for keeping me excited about the future
and motivated to share my
knowledge with your generation.

# Acknowledgments

Compared to the effort expended and the lessons learned writing my first book, compiling the information for this book was fairly easy. I used many of the ideas and material from *Lasting Wealth Is A Matter Of Timing*, updated it to the present, and formatted it in a way that I believe is easier for the average investor to understand.

Therefore, most of my obligations and indebtedness are to those who first urged me to enter the investment management field and provided me opportunities along the way, those whose counsel sparked the ideas that formed the foundation of my investment philosophy, and those who encouraged me to persevere in the face of traditional skepticism. If you wonder if I was thinking of you when you read this, I was and sincerely thank you. Most of all, I am grateful to the loyal clients who possessed the discipline and patience to stick with me through the years. Without you, there would be no story to tell.

I also owe a debt of gratitude to Rick Maturi, coauthor on my first book, a true professional and a really nice guy. If it weren't for Rick, I would have never completed my first book, much less have taken on this project to write a second book.

Investment professionals Steve Blumenthal, Linda Ferentchak, Hays Glover, Steve Gradeless, Joe Ludwig, John Lyons, Peter Mauthe, Louis Mayberg, Paul Merriman, Roger Schreiner, Steve Shellans, and

Jerry Wagner were kind enough to review portions of the manuscript, spot errors, and offer constructive comments and suggestions. The errors that remain are, of course, my own.

My wife, LaGayle, and my daughter and talented coauthor, Kori, both shared the excitement, labor, and tension of this project . . . and still had encouraging words to offer. To both of you . . . my heartfelt thanks and my love!

—John K. Sosnowy

# About the Author

**John K. Sosnowy**

John K. Sosnowy is president of Sosnowy Investment Management Company (SIMCO), vice-president and portfolio manager of Flexible Plan Investments, Ltd., and chairman and CEO of SIMCO Financial, a member of the National Association of Security Dealers, Inc. During his decades of investment management experience, Sosnowy has been a nationally recognized pioneer in tactical asset allocation/risk management strategies. He is the founder and a past president of the Society of Asset Allocators and Fund Timers, Inc. (SAAFTI), an industry national trade association.

Sosnowy is a member of the American MENSA Society and holds a Bachelor of Science in Mathematics and a Master of Science in Industrial Engineering. His investment philosophy has been featured in *Forbes, Financial Planning, Investment Advisor, Newsweek, Research, Technical Analysis of Stocks & Commodities*, and many other national and regional publications. He has been a guest on Dan Rather's *CBS Evening News* and hosted *Money Talks*, an investment radio show.

His first book, *Lasting Wealth Is A Matter Of Timing*, written in 1996, is considered by many to be the definitive work in this field.

He resides with his bride of thirty-four years, LaGayle, in Houston, Texas, and Seattle, Washington.

## With Kori S. Voorhees

Kori S. Voorhees was marketing coordinator for Sosnowy Investment Management Company, Inc. (SIMCO) for three years before embarking on a full-time writing career. Her first novel, *Christmas on Wednesday*, was published in 2002.

Voorhees received her Bachelor of Arts in Business Administration with a Marketing concentration from the University of Washington. She lives with her husband, Colby, in Seattle, Washington.

# Table of Contents

Introduction ...............................................................17
MYTH #1:    If I make a high income, I'll be rich. ...............21
MYTH #2:    My home can make me rich. .............................28
MYTH #3:    Collectibles are great investments. ...................32
MYTH #4:    If I never take any stock market risk, I can't lose. . 35
MYTH #5:    Simply buying and holding several good stocks or
            a good common stock mutual fund over the long
            haul is the best way to invest. ...........................39
MYTH #6:    Individual stocks are better investments than
            mutual funds. ...............................................55
MYTH #7:    Dollar cost averaging takes the risk out of "buy
            and hold" investing. .......................................58
MYTH #8:    The stock market is a random walk. No one can
            predict what it is going to do. ..........................62
MYTH #9:    Asset allocation reduces risk and increases
            returns. .......................................................67
MYTH #10:   Invest in what you know or where you work. ...78
MYTH #11:   Time in the market, not market timing, is the key
            to investment success. ....................................83
MYTH #12:   Market timing is a relatively new investment
            strategy without proven results. .......................95
MYTH #13:   The stock market can be counted on to make me
            10-12 percent per year. ................................. 101
MYTH #14:   I'll never make any money in a down market. .. 104
MYTH #15:   With the information available to me today, I
            don't need professional advice. I can do it
            myself. ...................................................... 108
MYTH #16:   After no more than one year, I should be able to

evaluate whether my investment approach is
working or not. ............................................... 120

MYTH #17: Variable annuities are for fools. ....................... 126

MYTH #18: This time it's different. .................................. 140

MYTH #19: There is a "Holy Grail" in investing . . . I just
need to find it! ................................................ 147

Epilogue ....................................................... 152

Appendix A ....................................................... 155

Appendix B ....................................................... 159

Appendix C ....................................................... 161

Appendix D ....................................................... 164

Appendix E ....................................................... 167

Glossary ....................................................... 173

Index ....................................................... 193

# Introduction

The main goal in my first book, *Lasting Wealth Is A Matter of Timing*, written in 1996, was to spread the risk management gospel to many thousands of investors in time to protect them and to save their wealth from the effects of the next devastating bear market which I saw looming over the horizon. As I stated then, "The days of the current roaring bull market are numbered. You can quote me on that. Sooner or later , the big bullish wave in stock prices will end and come crashing down . . . . Unless investor attitudes change dramatically, I predict that hanging on blindly, or buying the dip, in the hope of a price rebound will be the downfall of many baby boomers and disastrous to their retirement years. That is what I hope to prevent by writing this book."

The good news is that since 1996 thousands and thousands of investors did get the message in time to protect themselves from the worst of the stock market debacle that has occurred since 2000. Depending on which active risk management strategy or strategies they utilized, some fared better than others. But I believe it is safe to say that almost anyone who followed the suggestions in my book is better off today than if he or she followed the old traditional buy and hold strategy during the same period of time.

Unfortunately, you may be one of the hundreds of thousands of investors, maybe even millions, who did not get the message in time. This book, *Everything You Know About Investing Is Wrong*, is written for you. The purpose of this book is not to tout me as the world's greatest money manager, nor is it to convince you to hire any firm I am affiliated with to manage your money. When I give you a phone number or a website address, it is simply to assist you in gathering more information and/or prospectuses. It is not a recommendation of any firm or strategy. My goals for this book are to dispel some of the most common myths about investing, to share with you what I have learned in over thirty years of investment management experience, and to give you hope for your future investment success. Of course, probably not everything you know about investing is wrong; however, a majority of what you think you know may be wrong . . . which makes this book worthwhile for you.

The first three myths set the stage for the rest of the book. In Myth #1, I will explain the important differences between accumulating wealth and retaining wealth and give you some suggestions for planning for a worry-free retirement. In Myths #2 and #3, I will dispel the notion that simply investing in your home or in collectibles will make you rich. The remainder of the book is devoted to debunking many of the most popular myths about stock market investing and to giving you a blueprint for successful investing.

Do *not* give up on the stock market! I know that's what many of you are tempted to do right now after the results of the past few years, but it is not what you should be doing. I believe that there will be some great wealth-building times in the coming decade. Don't miss out by hiding your dollars under a mattress. Instead, learn from your mistakes, and you will be a much more successful investor in the future. I believe that anyone can do it. Even janitors have retired leaving million dollar estates to charity. You do not have to make a big income. You just have to be able to separate the myth from the fact.

There is a good quote attributed to Frank Williams, a successful stock investor of the early 20th century that I believe is still appropriate today: "The market is most dangerous when it looks best; it is most inviting when it looks worst." Wow, you are probably thinking, it must be really inviting right now. Sure, for the *long* term. Our research says that once the stock market has declined by 40 percent or more from a bull market high, long-term returns on equities have been very rewarding. But in the interim we could still have further declines and possibly even years and years of a trading range type market before those attractive long-term returns are realized.

The problem for too many investors is that they do not have the discipline and patience to stick with stocks through those frustrating interim periods. Instead, they swear off stocks close to the bottom, only to return years later close to the next market top.

There are many ways to invest in the stock market that can work. But I have found that active risk management is one of the few investment methods that is logical, emotionally compatible with our human temperment, and fits our return/risk needs. That is why I hope to convince you before you finish reading this book that utilizing a disciplined risk management strategy can help you reduce your drawdowns enough during bear market periods to keep you committed to equity investing and thereby benefitting from the market's superior returns over time.

Good reading and successful investing!

# MYTH #1

## If I make a high income, I'll be rich.

"For age and want save while you may. No morning sun lasts a whole day."

—*Ben Franklin*

"How much money you accumulate by retirement will depend upon three things: when you start saving, how much you manage to save each year, and how much your investments return over the long run. Of the three, how soon you start saving turns out to be the most important."

—*George Shaffner*
*The Arithmetic of Life*

Unfortunately, accumulating wealth and retaining wealth are two very different matters. Look at the entertainers and athletes who earn millions and millions and have nothing to show for it after their careers have ended. A high income just means you are bringing significant dollars in the door. It only translates into real wealth if you spend less than you make after taxes each year and invest the difference wisely. I would not consider someone to be rich until they possessed the investment assets necessary to generate enough income to live comfortably without having to work to supplement their income.

## Real Wealth 101

Seeking "real wealth" first requires an understanding of what constitutes real wealth. Use the following definitions and comments as a solid framework for developing your plan and strategies to create lasting wealth.

**Budget.** A spending plan for living "below your means." Target spending as little as necessary on consumption items (entertainment, vacations, etc.) and things that depreciate in value (clothing, cars, consumer electronics, etc.) by comparing prices and ferreting out discounts. This way you can save and invest as much as possible in items that can appreciate (mutual funds, stocks, real estate, etc.) to increase your net worth.

Use credit cards only for convenience and never as a way to obtain credit, because the exorbitant interest charges will eat you alive. For example, assume you charge $2,500 on your credit card at 19.8 percent APR and pay only the required minimum payment of 2 percent of the balance due. It would take you 53.4 years to pay off the balance and over that 53 years you would have paid a total of $13,057. That amounts to $10,577 in interest on purchases of $2,500. Not a very savvy way to accumulate wealth.

One way to boost your net worth is to budget and live below your means. Shopping at discount stores, purchasing less flashy automobiles, clipping coupons, and taking sack lunches to work versus eating at trendy dining establishments all put money in the bank and to work in investments, compounding your income. This habit requires creating a mental attitude of saving and investing over spending.

**Compound Interest.** The process of earning interest on interest over time (a miracle) or paying interest on interest over time (a curse). For example, if you invested $400 a month for 30 years at 8 percent interest, your nest egg would grow to $596,144 due to the miracle of compounding. Likewise, paying $400 per month for 30 years for a home mortgage at 8 percent interest would result in total payments of $144,400, of which, $89,486 would represent interest charges.

**Income.** The money you receive each week, month, or year from employment or investments. Income is taxed, net worth is not. Which makes more sense to try to maximize?

**Net Worth.** Also considered real wealth. The difference between what you earn and what you spend each year (i.e. what you save) represents your annual addition to net worth. You can invest this difference in assets such as certificates of deposit, stocks, bonds, mutual funds, etc. and ultimately make yourself rich through the miracle of compounding. You calculate net worth by deducting total liabilities from total assets.

Concentrate on building net worth. One savings and investment formula recommends saving 5 percent of after-tax income until age 40. At that point, you add 1 percentage point annually until age 45. From then on, you save at least 10 percent annually and continue to build up your savings and investments, even into retirement.

Obviously, these regular savings require putting into action a financial plan. Put your retirement plans such as 401(k)'s, IRA's, and SEP's to work for you on a tax-deferred basis. Investigate other financial planning options such as insurance, variable annuities, and direct investments such as stocks, bonds, and mutual funds. Many people fail to take full advantage of their tax-deferred 401(k) plans. Adding $1,000 per year to your contribution only costs you $720 (assuming you are in the 28 percent tax bracket). Over 25 years, that amounts to $18,000 (25 x 720) out of your spending money. However, assuming an 8 percent compounded rate of return, you will retire with an extra $52,600 after 25 years.

As a guide, Thomas J. Stanley and William D. Danko, authors of *The Millionaire Next Door*, devised the following net worth equation. Multiply one-tenth of your age by your annual income to determine the approximate level of your desired net worth. For example, if you are currently 25 years of age and earn $40,000 annually, your net worth should be $100,000 (25 x .1 x $40,000). The difference between your target net worth and actual net worth lets you know how much more you need to save to close the gap.

**Rich.** The circumstance of possessing enough assets (bank deposits, investments, income producing property, etc.) to generate sufficient income to live comfortably without having to work to supplement your income. As a young single person today, maybe $2,500 a month is sufficient income to live comfortably. If so, you might need $1,000,000 in capital to generate enough income to maintain your purchasing power by the time your working years are over.

Project yourself 20 years into the future. You are now married with three children. In the meantime, inflation has increased at 4 percent annually. At that rate, your income level must increase to around $7,000 per month just to keep up with the higher cost of living and the additional costs of raising a family. In order to generate that level of income and protect against future inflation, you will need approximately $2.5 million in assets. At retirement age, it would take even more, an estimated $3.5 million to $4 million.

**Success.** The achievement of finding something you like to do so much that you would be happy to do it for nothing. Learn how to perform your work so well that others will pay you for doing it . . . then you are a success. Utilize all your potential . . . be all you can be.

When considering a job, follow your heart, not your pocketbook. Search for the career that you truly love. Don't worry about low initial compensation. Look to the future and look for ways to improve yourself and, in the process, achieve greater job satisfaction and higher compensation.

Accumulating lasting wealth takes a concerted effort and advance planning. I recommend the following steps for a more satisfying retirement.

1. Develop a reasonable long-term plan and stick with it. View proper planning for worry-free retirement from a long-term perspective. Set your objectives and employ a professional investment manager (see Myth #15). Make changes only in response to significant changes in your circumstances or consistent underachievement of objectives over a complete economic cycle (five to ten years). By instituting a plan, you will be less likely to be tempted to react emotionally to short-run fluctuations in investment markets (see Myth #16).

2. Be honest in assessing your ability and willingness to take risk. In order to beat taxes

and inflation, you must accept some risk. But do not let greed outweigh good investment judgement in determining the proper reward/risk ratio for your financial situation and desired risk posture.

3. Cultivate living habits that favor saving, and ultimately investing, over spending.

4. Let the miracle of compound interest work over time. The active risk management approach to investing has proven that it has the potential to generate superior returns versus both risk-free investments and the overall market over the long-term, especially on a risk-adjusted basis. You will learn more about active risk management in Myths #5, 7, 8, 11, 12, 18, and the Epilogue.

5. Entrust your retirement assets to investment professionals. Unless you possess the experience, personal self-discipline, and willingness to manage your retirement assets full-time, I strongly suggest that you hire a professional investment advisor, registered with the SEC under the Investment Advisors Act of 1940 (see Myth #15). The roster of SAAFTI* (www.saafti.com) members is a good source of potential candidates.

Why worry about day-to-day market fluctuations when you have an experienced, full-time professional tracking market moves for you? Keeping your investment plan on track is like keeping your car finely tuned . . . for most people, you cannot do it yourself anymore. You need to go to the professionals for expertise. Like the automobile repair advertisement says, "You can pay me now or pay me later." If you do not take care to fine-tune your investments, you could pay dearly in poor performance and devastating bear market losses at an inopportune time.

*\* SAAFTI, the Society of Asset Allocators and Fund Timers, Inc., is the national trade association of registered investment advisors who utilize active investment management strategies to manage client assets.*

**"PREPARE—It wasn't raining when Noah built the ark."**

*—Author Unknown*

## Key Points to Remember:

- Someone that earns a high income is not necessarily rich.
- Someone that is rich possesses enough assets to generate sufficient income to live comfortably without having to work to supplement their income.
- Accumulating lasting wealth takes a concerted effort and advance planning.

# MYTH #2

## My home can make me rich.

"You have to live somewhere. So even if you sell your home, it won't help support you unless you buy a cheaper place and stash the profits elsewhere."

*—Harold Evensky*
*Financial Planner*

According to the August 31, 2002, issue of *The Economist*, there is nothing wrong with investing in housing, but some investors may now be putting too much faith in ever-rising property prices.

Just as with equities in the late 1990's, property bulls are now coming up with bogus arguments for why rampant house-price inflation is sure to continue. Demographic change is said to be permanently boosting demand. Physical restrictions and tough planning laws are said to be curtailing new supply. Similar arguments were heard in Japan in the late 1980's and Germany in the early 1990's—and yet in recent years, housing prices in these two countries have been falling. British housing prices also tumbled in the late 1980's. The truth is that housing prices, like equities, cannot for long outpace the growth of nominal incomes.

In another article in the same issue, *The Economist* says that there is a big risk that investors, burned by the stock market, are now over-investing in housing. The market for housing is almost as prone to irrational exuberance as the stock market. And a housing bubble is more dangerous than a stock market bubble, because it is associated with more debt. A steep fall in housing prices would harm the global economy far more than a slump in share prices.

The best gauge of whether housing prices are overvalued is a ratio of house prices to average disposable income—the equivalent, as it were, of the price/earnings ratio for stock shares. In the United States, this ratio is now close to its peak of the late 1980's.

The real housing bubble in the United States is not the rise in house prices, but the growth in mortgage debt, which is at record levels in relation to incomes. Home buyers may be underestimating the true cost of housing. Interest rates are low because inflation is low, but that means that borrowers can no longer rely on inflation to erode their debts, as it did in the past.

At the very least, households hoping that ever-rising house prices will provide generous nest eggs are likely to be disappointed. At worst, the risk is that prices in many countries may take a tumble.

From 1998 to 2001, single-family home prices rose an average of 8.2 percent a year nationally. As a result, many Americans have come to view real estate as a more secure path to wealth than the stock market, taking out ever-bigger mortgages and trading up as quickly as possible. While owning a house provides substantial financial benefits, you should not count on home ownership to make you rich.

An article in the July 2002 issue of *Money* ex-

plains why putting money in your home is no substitute for saving and investing. The key reason is
that a house represents a much different type of
wealth than a stock portfolio does. For one thing, it
does not have good liquidity—it cannot be converted
to cash with a phone call. It takes time to sell a
house—and you cannot be sure of its actual value
until you find a buyer.

More importantly, as investment advisor Harold
Evensky points out, you have to live somewhere. So
even if you sell your home, it will not help support
you unless you buy a cheaper place and stash the
profits elsewhere. And for the most part, even retirees do not cash out unless they are forced to. Most
retirees prefer to stay where they are, while others
may move to retirement communities or condos that
cost as much as their former homes.

"Most real estate economists are not looking for
a crash, but there's bound to be a softening of prices,"
says Mark Zandi, chief economist at the West
Chester, Pennsylvania, research firm, Economy.com.
"And over the long run, you can't expect prices to
rise much faster than people's incomes, since that
would make homes unaffordable." To sum it up,
economist Karl Case states, "The best reason to buy
a home is because it is something you enjoy—over
the long term, it will probably be a good investment,
but it won't make you rich."

Robert R. Prechter, Jr. agrees with this assessment in his new book, *Conquer the Crash*. After the
stock experience of 2000-02, people are saying,
"Maybe stocks can come down for a few months from
time to time, but real estate won't; real estate never
has." They are saying it because real estate is the
last thing still soaring at the top of the great asset
mania, but it, too, will fall if there is a deflationary

depression. Property values collapsed along with the depression of the 1930's. Few know that many values associated with property—such as rents—continued to fall through most of the 1940's, even after stocks had recovered substantially.

The worst thing about real estate is its lack of liquidity during a bear market. At least in the stock market, when your stock is down 60 percent and you realize you've made a horrendous mistake, you can call your broker and get out. With real estate, you can't pick up the phone and sell. You need to find a buyer for your house in order to sell it. In a real estate bust, buyers just go away. Enjoy living in your home, but do not count on it to finance your retirement.

## Key Points to Remember:

- Putting money in your home is no substitute for investing.
- Investing in a home is very different from investing in the stock market. A home does not have good liquidity, meaning that it cannot be converted to cash quickly.
- House prices, like equities, cannot for long outpace the growth of nominal incomes.
- The market for housing is almost as prone to irrational exuberance as the stock market.
- Households hoping that ever-rising house prices will provide generous nest eggs are likely to be disappointed.
- You have to live somewhere. Even if you sell your home, it will not help support you unless you buy a cheaper place and stash the profits elsewhere.

# MYTH #3

## Collectibles are great investments.

**"Collecting trends are usually fads. And fads usually fade."**

*—John K. Sosnowy*

Collecting purely for investment purposes usually proves to be foolish. The chances of losing money when the collectibility factor is priced into an item are enormous. Collecting trends are usually fads. And fads usually fade.

Even art goes through cycles. The Japanese investors who bought paintings at record prices a decade ago have lost much of the value of their purchases.

There are times when collecting might make sense. When I was a kid, I collected U.S. coins and baseball cards. You could find rare coins in everyday pocket change. My uncle was our local church treasurer and allowed me to sort through the church's weekly take of coins and exchange them one for one. I also counted all the change and rolled it for deposit at the bank for him. There was *no downside* to the hobby because the coins were always worth at least face value.

When I started my baseball card collection, I was

certain I was going to get rich from my investment of five cents for a pack of baseball cards. Of course, I was wrong. My collection did increase in value over the years and it was something that I enjoyed doing, but it wasn't going to make me rich. Even worse, my mother accidentally threw out my cards when house-cleaning many years later, so I wasn't even able to pass my collection on to my daughter.

Much of the 50's memorabilia and other baby-boomer collectibles are probably at an all-time high in value. For many supposed collectibles, such as Beanie Babies and such, it's already too late. Bobblehead dolls probably won't be far behind. For most people, even if you assume that your collectibles appreciate greatly in value, they do not become a great investment because you never convert them to cash. You keep them and pass them on. The purpose of "investing" is to generate future income for retire-ment, educating kids, etc.

Many people believe diamonds are the exception, but they are not. Diamonds may be a girl's best friend, but they were one of the poorest performing invest-ments ever in the first half of the 1980's when high quality diamonds depreciated six consecutive years a total of over 80 percent—an average per annum loss of 17 percent. Diamonds stabilized somewhat during the second half of the decade, rising about 3 percent per annum. During most of the 1990's, dia-monds did not even match the pace of inflation, ap-preciating just 1.36 percent annually, according to *Wiesenberger Investments Performance Digest*. Dia-monds have not only been volatile, but they have shown poor performance over the past 20+ years since the commodity boom of 1979-80. The myth about diamonds being a great investment has been just that, a myth.

In sum, know your collectibles, take good care of them, and most of all, enjoy them. But do not expect them to make you rich.

## Key Points to Remember:

· Collectibles are generally not good investments.
· Collect for pleasure, not for profit.
· It is not a good investment if you don't ever sell and use the proceeds as an income-generating asset.

# MYTH #4

## If I never take any stock market risk, I can't lose.

"It's important to distinguish between certainty and safety. Certainty is having someone guarantee you the same number of dollars at some point in the future. Safety is the accretion of purchasing power after taxes and inflation, so you don't outlive your money."

*—Nick Murray*

Connie Conservative (a fictional character, though her situation is not) retired in 1973 with a nest egg of $100,000 to invest. She determined that she needed to withdraw $8,000 (adjusted for inflation) annually for living expenses and as a supplement to her social security benefits.

She chose to invest $50,000 in a portfolio of safe U.S. T-Bills and $50,000 in long-term government bonds. For analysis purposes she could have just as easily invested in certificates of deposit and money market funds. Her primary concern was for the safety of her hard-earned money, remembering that her parents had lost everything during the Depression. While Connie truly believed her actions were prudent, she was setting herself up for financial disaster.

As the amount withdrawn each year increased
due to the inflation adjustment, the value of her
portfolio decreased. By 1983, her bond nest egg dis-
appeared. By 1986, the T-Bills followed suit, and
she was completely broke and forced to move in with
her daughter's family to live out her golden years.

| Connie Conservative | |
| --- | --- |
| Amount Invested: | $100,000 |
| Total Amount Withdrawn | |
| through 12/31/1986: | $154,915 |
| Portfolio Value | |
| As of 12/31/1986: | $—0— |
| Financial Status: | Flat Broke |

Since interest rates are much lower today than
when Connie Conservative retired, her nest egg would
most likely disappear even quicker if she had been
retiring today.

**"Building your personal wealth without consid-
ering inflation risk represents a head-in-the-sand
attitude. It's not how many dollars you have but
what those dollars will purchase that's important."**

*—Paul Merriman*

As stated by William E. Donoghue in *Donoghue's
Mutual Fund Super Stars*, "America simply does not
have time to play it safe with retirement savings,
and with the changes in the investment markets;
'playing it safe' may be the riskiest strategy of all.
The risk of not only having insufficient savings but
of losing those savings to the 'safety' of the fixed
income markets is dramatic . . . ."

" . . . My examination into nearly two centuries of financial data reveals . . . over the long run the returns on stocks are so stable that stocks are actually *safer* than either government bonds or Treasury Bills. The constancy of the long-term, after-inflation returns on stocks was truly astonishing, while the return on fixed income assets posed higher risks for the long-term investor."

*—Jeremy J. Siegel, Professor of Finance*
*The Wharton School, University of Pennsylvania*
*Stocks for the Long Run*

Siegel's study should convince most investors that stocks are the best asset class to use in an effective investment strategy over the long haul. However, years of experience and the bear market of 2000-02 have shown that you cannot usually get investors to buy and hold common stocks through major bear market declines of 30 percent or 40 percent or more. Since bear markets are a fact of life, this poses a real dilemma. How can I keep investors committed to an equities-oriented investment strategy over the long haul in order to achieve their financial objectives? During my more than thirty years in the investment business, I have found only one practical solution, reducing risk through an active risk management investment strategy. You'll find more information on the value of active risk management in the chapters that follow.

" . . . the biggest financial risk is not taking any risk at all."

*—John C. Bogle*
*Founder and Former Chairman, The Vanguard*
*Fund Group*

## Key Points to Remember:

- You can lose it all while taking no stock market risk at all.
- When you retire, you cannot afford to let your money retire too!
- Too much investment conservatism can lead to catastrophe.
- Reducing risk, not avoiding risk, is the key to achieving your financial objectives.

# MYTH #5

## Simply buying and holding several good stocks or a good common stock mutual fund over the long haul is the best way to invest.

**"To buy when others are despondently selling and to sell when others are avidly buying requires the greatest fortitude and pays the greatest rewards."**

—*Sir John Templeton*

### Debunking Buy and Hold Strategies

True or false? Over the long run, the stock market has outperformed virtually all other investments, so buying and holding stocks represents the best investment strategy.

False. Don't be fooled by this faulty conclusion, even though the underlying assumption is fact. It is true that stock market investments have outperformed all other classes of investment alternatives over the long run; however, sitting on stocks while a bear market like the one that began in March 2000 erodes the value of your investment portfolio can be catastrophic to your financial well-being. This is especially true if you don't have time to wait for a market rebound to recapture ground lost during the decline.

Employing a buy and hold strategy takes time to work, sometimes extraordinary amounts of time. It takes a strong stomach and tremendous emotional discipline that the vast majority of investors do not possess. Buy and hold is definitely a young person's game and may not even represent the best strategy for them.

If you are at or near retirement, a buy and hold strategy may be one of the riskiest approaches to the market you could take. Assume you invested $100,000 in the S&P 500 in January 1973. Within 21 months your portfolio would have shrunk to $51,800, a loss of over 48 percent.

In 1973, the market lost ground nine out of twelve months, closing out the year with a 21.5 percent loss for large company stocks. The following year accelerated the decline with a loss of 34.4 percent in the value of large company stocks. October was the only month to deliver a positive return in 1974. It would have taken seven and one-half years to recoup your bear market loss, over 12 years when you factor in the effects of inflation. I don't know many retirees who could withstand a seven year period, much less 12 years, without earnings on their investments and still enjoy the quality of life they desire.

From March 2000 to September 2002, the S&P 500 declined 46 percent and the NASDAQ Index declined 77 percent. Who knows how long it will take investors who have suffered these losses to recover!

Academics, including Nobel laureate economist Paul Samuelson at the Massachusetts Institute of Technology, argue that the longer you have your money invested in the stock market, the greater the probability you will suffer devastating losses in a crash or series of crashes. Therefore, the buy and hold strategy makes your retirement funds susceptible to such crashes. Active risk management strategies aim to help you miss the brunt of those crashes.

There's another major fallacy in the buy and hold strategy expounded by so-called market pundits. Despite the proclamation and even the determination of investors to stick to their buy and hold guns, in practice many bail out as dramatic stock price plunges become simply unbearable. One of the largest redemption periods followed the crash of 1987 when the market was down. Many of these so-called buy and hold investors then missed out on the market rebound and the great bull market of the 1990's. Likewise, some of the largest mutual funds sales periods consisted of the months leading up to market highs. Other high/low periods reveal the same pattern.

Would-be buy and hold investors listen to media reports of stock price plunges and record stock market declines and head for the doors. Emotions take over the reins from rationally thought out long-term investment plans. They become emotional asset allocators instead of tactical asset allocators. Savvy investors would be wise to forget the buy and hold strategy with its accompanying emotional seesaw and employ active risk management strategies in its place. While active risk management may not work for amateurs without discipline, it can work at the hand of a professional manager!

Money manager Paul Merriman (www.merrimancapital.com) points out the psychology at work today. While many profess to be dedicated buy and hold investors, they lack the true commitment to stick with it. This behavior reflects today's

society. Merriman uses marriage as an excellent example. Both people enter into a contract or commitment believing that they won't change their minds
later. Yet marriage, like investing, goes through some
difficult times over the years. When the pain reaches
a certain threshold, many people bail out as testi-
fied by the divorce statistics for the United States.
Despite most people's honest intentions, many will
also abandon the buy and hold strategy when the
pain level gets too high.

Bear markets are no fun to be around, and they
require a long time to get over. After the 86 percent
market drop that began in 1929, twenty years later
the market still stood a full 58 percent below its
1929 peak. More recently, sixteen years after the 45
percent drop in the Dow Jones Industrial Average
that began in 1966 the Dow still traded 22 percent
below its peak. Today, the Japanese stock market is
still 76 percent *below* its all-time high in 1989.

## The Fallacy of the Mountain Chart

Many of you have probably seen the "mountain
charts" in mutual fund advertising showing that
$10,000 invested years and years ago in XYZ fund
would now be worth hundreds of thousands of dollars, maybe even millions. Upon closer examination,
you will see that climbing the investment mountain,
like climbing a major peak, is fraught with danger.
It is not an easy venture. First of all, savvy mountain climbers don't go straight up for fear of plum-
meting to disaster. The same holds true in the investment world. In both environments, you are likely
to encounter some grizzly bears and other challenges
along the way. The advice to simply buy and hold
stocks and sit back while you accumulate a moun-

tain of wealth simply does not hold up under close scrutiny. Remember, nothing goes up in a straight line.

While the long-term trend may be successively higher, you will encounter periodic price pullbacks and even major down markets as we had from the spring of 2000 to the fall of 2002. They are a fact of life in the investment world. Just as the mountain climber retraces his or her steps to maneuver around a difficult obstacle or avoid a dangerous situation, the investor must learn how to deal with and avoid major market retracements that can prove devastating to your portfolio and your accumulation of wealth. It is crucial to protect yourself against those inevitable down markets.

There is an old saying that, "The only things certain in life are death and taxes." I would like to amend that truism to add the certainty of declining markets. You can be sure that declining markets and even brutal bear markets will continue to plague investors in the years to come.

This is not a new idea. Way back in the August 15, 1969 issue of the *Forbes Mutual Fund Survey*, the editors issued the following warning, which holds just as true today:

" . . . don't listen to the salesman who tells you not to worry about *down* markets because the big trend is up. Maybe the big trend *is* up, but the intermediate downs aren't necessarily little ones. And sometimes people are *forced* to sell during the downs. Sure, their stocks will go up again, but somebody else will own them. For few, if any, humans is downside risk a matter of no concern."

Attempting to build a mountain of wealth via the buy and hold strategy contains major risks. To illustrate, consider the results of the following buy and hold strategy calculated with historical data. In this example, we used the NYSE TR Index, which includes every NYSE stock equally weighted and including dividends, as a proxy for the performance results of a typical stock portfolio.

Assume you invested $100,000 in a buy and hold strategy from January 1, 1970 to June 30, 2002. Your investment would have delivered a net annual return of 12 percent and your $100,000 initial investment would have grown to over $3.9 million by the end of June 2002 as shown in Chart 5-1.

## Chart 5-1

PERFORMANCE SUMMARY

|  | Net Annual Return | $100,000 Investment Value 6/30/2002 |
| --- | --- | --- |
| Buy and Hold NYSE | 12.00% | $3,925,088 |

*NYSE=New York Stock Exchange Total Return Index*
*$100,000 invested 01/01/1970*

On the surface the accumulated $3.9 million mountain and net annual return of 12 percent looks attractive. However, as you climbed up the NYSE mountain, you were beaten back in excess of 53 percent during the bear market of April 14, 1972 through September 13, 1974. Similarly, if you were an investor in the high-flying Fidelity Magellan Fund during that same time frame, you would have had to survive a drop of over 58 percent before reaching the top of the mountain. The results are even more dramatic if you had invested in the Evergreen S4 (small companies) Fund. The bear would have devoured over 73 percent of your assets at the depth of that bear market. The critical question is . . . would you really have kept climbing to reach the top of the mountain? Or would you have opted to bail out to save what little remained of your portfolio assets? I doubt that you would have kept climbing! Most investors do not have the fortitude to continue to endure continuing pain with no hope of a turnaround in sight. They bail out and lock in their staggering losses, just as they have done again since 2000 with the high-tech funds.

**"It's human nature to be influenced by the actions of the crowd, particularly in emotionally charged settings . . . . The crowd behaves the same way in every market cycle. Some trends last longer than others and some travel farther than others, but the psychological progression through each bull and bear market is always the same."**

*—Robert R. Prechter, Jr.*

**" . . . The bulging files sum up a fascinating history, offering surprising evidence that the stock market has changed not a whit in the last century. Only its price history . . . . There have been no significant changes in the market, as opposed to the marketplace . . . . What all those stock tables and tales, books, and charts illustrate is an endless repetition of psychological patterns . . . ."**

*—John Dennis Brown*
*101 Years on Wall Street*

## The Ideal Investment

So what is the answer? The "ideal investment" is one which earns enough return to offset the effects of inflation and taxes, and still allows you to sleep comfortably at night. The goal is to accumulate a nest egg capable of generating a level of earnings you cannot outlive! This should be accomplished within a framework of risk reduction. Additionally, the ideal investment would provide liquidity and be eligible for use in tax-deferred accounts such as IRA's and 401(k)'s. Historically, the investment closest to that ideal has been equities, but buy and hold investing in the stock market with its periodic price declines and bear markets may not let you sleep at night.

I believe a strategy that serves investors better is what I call active risk management, which encompasses tactical asset allocation, dynamic asset allocation, and market timing. The goal of active risk management is 180 degrees different from emotional investing that gets investors into and out of investments at the wrong times. Through the disciplined use of time-tested econometric models, active risk managers attempt to be in a position to purchase stocks when the emotional investors are selling and sell stocks when the emotional investors are buying.

Conclusion: Real world results for over thirty years (see Chart 12-1) as well as hypothetical computer simulations since 1927 for a model as currently formulated (see Chart 5-2) have shown that active risk management can accomplish its goal of reducing losses in the worst markets and nearly matching the big gain performances of buy and hold strategies in the best markets.

# Chart 5-2

PERFORMANCE SUMMARY
4/8/1927 to 6/30/2002

| | Comp. Annual Return | Net Annual Return | $100,000 Inv. Now Worth | Volatility 'Beta' | Risk Adj. Superiority Index 'Alpha' |
|---|---|---|---|---|---|
| MANAGED (NYSE) | 19.40% | 18.50% | 35,416,538,866 | 0.433 | 11.842 |
| | | | | | |
| Buy and Hold (NYSE) | | 12.20% | 569,890,000 | 1.08 | 1.272 |

*Courtesy of SIMCO*
*NYSE=New York Stock Exchange Total Return Index*
*Past model research results should in no way be construed as a guarantee of future return.*
*See Appendix A for Disclosure Statement*

## Closet Market Timers

There are a number of well known investment professionals who claim not to believe in active risk management. No matter what they call themselves, I contend that their actions make them out to be "closet" market timers. Many stock market gurus expound buy and hold strategies, but close analysis reveals they practice more active management. Analysis of the actions of legendary investors reveals that their strategies often rely on the basic principles of market timing and that active risk management does indeed work.

At one time or another, Warren Buffett, Peter Lynch, John C. Bogle, and other investing heroes of the day have urged ordinary investors not to attempt to time the market, stating that market timing does not work. But do their own investment philosophies match their words?

Not really. Fidelity says that you should buy and hold, yet they invented sector funds which encourage market timing. A recent Fidelity Brokerage Ser-

vices, Inc. advertisement proclaims, "The right idea
at the right time . . . for 50 years." Yet they say they
do not believe in active risk management or market
timing.

It is interesting to note that Warren Buffett, often quoted as the ultimate buy and hold investor,
decided in 1969 that the market as a whole was
overpriced and opted to sell. In his book, *Warren
Buffett, The Good Guy of Wall Street*, author Andrew
Kilpatrick quotes a letter from Buffett to his partners stating that the investing environment was becoming more negative and frustrating. When Buffett
liquidated the Buffett Partnership in 1969 (after ring-
ing up a 29.5 percent annual compounded return
versus 7.4 percent for the Dow Jones Industrial Average), Buffett offered to help former partners make
"bond" investments.

Buffett's concern about market conditions and
his timing in exiting the market kept the partnership from suffering the slow market decline that cul-
minated in the bear market of 1973-74. In the midst
of the 1973-74 bear market, Buffett returned to equity investments, stating that there were just too
many good bargains to pass up. Unlike buy and hold
investors, he had no losses to recoup. His capital
was intact due to his excellent sense of market timing.

Buffett has acclaimed *The Intelligent Investor* by
Benjamin Graham as "by far the best book about
investing ever written." Included in Graham's classic investment book are such statements describing
market timing strategies as:

"According to tradition, the sound reason for increasing the percentage in common stocks would be
the appearance of the 'bargain price' levels created
in a protracted bear market. Conversely, sound pro-

cedure would call for reducing the common stock component below 50 percent when, in the judgement of the investor, the market has become dangerously high."

Benjamin Graham, Warren Buffett's mentor, is considered by many to be the most famous buy and hold investor of all time. The following excerpts and statistics come from *Benjamin Graham, Memoirs of the Dean of Wall Street*, written in 1964 and published in 1996 by McGraw Hill:

"The first half of 1929 went relatively well, but business started to fall off in the back half of the year . . . and the next three years were the worst of my career."

"In 1929, we closed the year with a loss of exactly 20 percent, which wasn't too bad considering the Dow was down considerably more than that . . . ."

" . . . despite an encouraging beginning, 1930 was the worst in the 33 year history of my fund management . . . our loss for 1930 was 50.5 percent. In 1931 we lost 16 percent . . . in 1932 we lost 3 percent . . . ."

"The cumulative losses for January 1929 through 1932 were 70 percent." And Graham was supposedly one of the greatest buy and hold investors of all time.

His own words tell the story of how hard the money would have to work just to get back to where he had been before 1929.

Malcolm S. Forbes, Jr. picked up on Buffett's market timing tendencies. Author Kirkpatrick quoted Forbes as saying, "We know Buffett as a value investor but I think he's a market timer, too . . . . We interviewed him (for *Forbes* magazine) in 1969 when he was a virtual unknown and he said the market was too high and that he was selling everything. We said, gosh, he sure called that one right. We inter-

viewed him again in 1974 when the market had declined two-thirds in value in real terms, after inflation. He said it was a time to buy and that he felt
like a sex-starved man in a harem."

In Peter Lynch's investment book, *Beating the
Market*, check out Peter's Principle #8. It's the only
exception to the general rule that owning stocks is
better than owning bonds as expressed by Lynch.
Principle #8 is provided below.

"When yields on long-term government bonds exceed the dividend yield on the S&P 500 by 6 percent
or more, sell your stocks and buy bonds."

Lynch goes on to explain that "I didn't buy bonds
for defensive purposes because I was afraid of
stocks . . . . I bought them because the yields exceeded the returns one could normally expect to get
from stocks." Another piece of timing advice from
Lynch is, "Buy shares when the stock price is at or
below the earnings line and not when the price line
diverges into the danger zone, well above the earnings line."

In his book, Lynch also offered advice that fits
well with a seasonal market timing strategy. "In the
late fall . . . annual tax-selling drives the prices of
smaller issues to pathetic lows . . . you could make
a nice living buying stocks from the low list in No-
vember and December during the tax-selling period
and holding them through January, when prices always seem to rebound."

Timing also played a role in Lynch's strategy with
Magellan Fund. "I divided the Magellan portfolio into
two parts: the small growth and cyclical stocks and
the conservative stocks. When the market heads
lower, I sell the conservative stocks and add to the
others. When the market picks up, I sell some of the
winners from the growth stocks and cyclical stocks

and add to the conservative stocks . . . . For brief periods at Magellan, I had 10 percent of the fund invested in utilites. Usually this happened when interest rates were declining and the economy was in a sputter. In other words, I treated the utilities as interest rate cyclicals and tried to time my entrances and my exits accordingly."

Other evidence of Lynch's closet market timer status is his statement in *Worth* magazine that, "On average every two years the market has a 10 percent decline. Every six years: 25 percent."

The following statement is attributed to John C. Bogle in his book, *Bogle on Mutual Funds, New Perspectives for the Intelligent Investor*. Bogle is the former chairman of the Vanguard Group of Investment Companies.

" . . . there is another approach, one that does not assure success but offers the prospect of extra returns at the margin, perhaps with less exposure to market risk. It is called tactical asset allocation . . . . One type of tactical allocation strategy involves changing the stock/bond ratio based on the relative outlooks for the respective financial markets."

Bogle hedges his statement by recommending placing severe restrictions on the extent of allocation changes, specifically varying by no more than 15 percentage points on either side. Thus, a portfolio would never have less than 35 percent nor more than 65 percent in stocks.

Even Sir John Templeton, the dean of mutual fund investing and master value hunter, employs market timing. In July 1993, Templeton urged investors to switch more into stocks and trim holdings of bonds. Later that year, Templeton shed his holdings in the Templeton Emerging Market Fund. When asked why he had not yet reinvested the money, Templeton replied, "There just didn't seem to be any hurry." In my book, that is market timing.

Paul C. Cabot, one of the founding fathers of the mutual fund industry, rounds out my list of prominent closet market timers. Cabot managed the State Street Investment Trust Fund during the Roaring Twenties, through the Stock Market Crash beginning in 1929, and through World War II. Cabot's fund survived a number of stock market crashes and earned an annual rate in excess of 13 percent from 1929 through 1948.

"As early as February 1928 we felt it wasn't safe to assume that the past four years of good returns would continue. Therefore, we did some selling ahead of time and turned into buyers when stocks became cheap (in the 1930s)," said Cabot.

State Street reduced its investment margin (leverage) in 1928 and 1929 and was 5 percent in cash by December 1929, moving to a 62 percent cash position by 1932. It didn't move back into equities until April 1933.

Cabot continually advised investors to use common sense and stick to fundamentals. He advocated avoiding market timing and using dollar cost averaging in their mutual fund investments. Cabot may have advised against market timing, but he practiced it at the most critical time in his career, 1929-33.

All of these men are considered legendary investors, investors who have proven their ability to outperform the markets. In addition, they approach the market with a level of information, knowledge, and intelligence that few investors can hope to match. Plus, each of them possess a strategy that they follow to determine not only when to buy, but when to sell. After all, buy and hold investing only makes sense when the reason you bought an investment still holds true today. As each of these investors have proved, selling at the right time is as important as buying at the right time.

Donald L. Cassidy, an analyst with Lipper Analytical Services, Inc. and a cum laude graduate of the Wharton School of Finance and Commerce at the University of Pennsylvania, covers this point well in his book, *It's Not What Stocks You Buy, It's When You Sell That Counts*. Like Cassidy, my goal is to help investors identify trouble early enough to cut losses before all that is left is false hope and a devastated portfolio.

**"It's my belief that every money manager, whether he or she professes to be or not, is a market timer. It's just that some managers' cycles are longer than others. Warren Buffett's cycle may be an extraordinary 20 years while Rich Paul's may be 20 days. Everyone else probably falls somewhere in between."**

*—John K. Sosnowy*

Market timing or, as we have called it, active risk management is a disciplined approach for reducing the risk of stock market investing. While the average investor may not be able to use active risk management due to the onset of emotional versus rational decision-making, active risk management can work in the hands of a disciplined professional, whether it be a Warren Buffett or a member of SAAFTI (www.saafti.com) that you hire to manage your personal investments. Don't let the confusion over the definition of active risk management or the naysayers, who have not been able to figure out how to use it properly, discourage you from evaluating its contributions to achieving solid risk-adjusted returns. You can

sit back with a buy and hold strategy and watch the
bear market chew up your portfolio or employ active
risk management strategies to reduce risk and conserve your portfolio assets for investment when the
market turns around.

## Key Points to Remember:

- Contrary to popular belief, buying and holding
  several stocks or common stock mutual funds
  over the long haul is one of the riskiest approaches to investing in the stock market that
  you could take.
- The longer you have your money invested in the
  stock market, the greater the probability you
  will suffer devastating losses in a crash or a
  series of crashes.
- Savvy investors would be wise to forget the buy
  and hold strategy with its accompanying emotional seesaw and employ disciplined risk
  management strategies in its place.
- The "ideal investment" is one which earns
  enough return to offset the effects of inflation
  and taxes, and still allows you to sleep comfortably at night.
- Many stock market gurus expound buy and
  hold strategies but close analysis reveals that
  they often practice some form of active risk
  management.
- Hiring an active risk management professional
  may be the most profitable investment decision
  you ever make because it will move you from
  an emotional to a rational decision-making
  process.

# MYTH #6

## Individual stocks are better investments than mutual funds.

"If you looked at a random selection of books on investing, it would be easy to conclude that by far the most important part of the problem is deciding how to pick the individual stocks that you hold in your portfolio. In fact, nothing could be more misleading . . . the crucial thing is not which stocks you pick, but whether you should hold stocks at all."

*—Andrew Smithers and Stephen Wright*
*Valuing Wall Street*

There are a number of reasons for using mutual funds versus individual securities to achieve your investment objectives. Mutual funds help create a diversified portfolio (reducing risk) at reasonable costs, feature professional investment management, and have good liquidity. And, with more mutual funds than stocks on the New York Stock Exchange from which to choose, why would you want to reinvent the wheel by building your own stock portfolio? Many experienced investment advisors leave the sector and stock picking to the fund manager and concentrate their efforts on correctly calling the primary trend of the market, which I estimate is 60 percent to 70 percent of the ballgame anyway.

In the March 2002 *Financial Planning* article entitled "Obscured By An Index," Craig Israelsen attempts to reveal some heretofore hidden information as he compares the performances of individual stocks and equity mutual funds. While there may be some survivorship bias in his numbers, I believe that his basic conclusions are valid.

He determined that over longer periods, mutual funds tend to insulate investors from loss more effectively than a random sample of individual stocks. For instance, over five years (ending December 31, 2001), only 4 percent of equity funds had a negative annualized return compared to 45 percent of individual stocks. Over the 10-year period (ending December 31, 2001), no equity funds had a negative annualized 10-year return while 634 stocks had a negative return.

When comparing performance between funds and stocks, a striking contrast emerges over the five-year period: The average equity fund produced an annualized return of 9.5 percent, compared to -1.9 percent for the average individual stock.

**"There is no escaping the conclusion that for retired investors, holding stocks on a continuous basis (buy and hold) is simply too risky."**

*—Andrew Smithers and Stephen Wright*
*Valuing Wall Street*

## Key Points to Remember:

· For most investors, mutual funds should be a better investment than individual stocks.

- Mutual funds deliver diversification and professional management.
- Over the long run, the vast majority of mutual funds have produced a positive return.
- In bear markets, individual stocks tend to hit lower lows more often than common stock mutual funds.

# MYTH #7

## Dollar cost averaging takes the risk out of "buy and hold" investing.

"Dollar cost averaging won't save you from a bear market."

*—John K. Sosnowy*
*Lasting Wealth Is A Matter Of Timing*

### Dollar Cost Averaging Debacle

Dollar cost averaging sends shivers down my spine if it is not accompanied by a disciplined risk control strategy. It is often touted as a safe way to invest through bear markets, as well as bull markets, with almost guaranteed success, without being a math guru or a Wall Street wizard.

It works like this. Over regular periodic intervals, the individual invests a set amount, such as $100 or $500 a month. According to dollar cost averaging advocates, over time, the investor tends to purchase shares at a low overall cost basis, which works to increase potential return. The investor purchases fewer shares when stock prices are high and more shares when stock prices are low. By spreading investments out over time, risk is also reduced.

That's the theory. It is a great approach in certain circumstances. For example, it allows beginning investors who only have a small amount to invest each month or quarter to develop a steady pattern of saving and investing. That is a lot better than not putting away any money at all. The real benefit of dollar cost averaging is that it forces the investor to save regularly.

For people looking to invest a lump sum disbursement or inheritance, it is a different story. If the market is in a relatively steady incline as it was in the 1990's, the dollar cost investor cannot make enough purchases at low prices to make the strategy worthwhile. Money not invested in stocks while the market is rising is not growing as fast as it could. Likewise, the value of dollar cost averaging diminishes over time. The amount an individual invested regularly ten or even five years ago won't keep pace with inflation. By my calculations, if you plan to use dollar cost averaging, you need to increase the amount you invest by at least ten percent each year.

But the real clincher that sinks dollar cost averaging in my mind is the prospect of a major market decline, such as we had from the spring of 2000 to the fall of 2002. As another form of the buy and hold strategy, dollar cost averaging leaves your portfolio open to significant erosion in the face of a bear market.

Early in a dollar cost averaging investment plan, a bear market does not do that much damage because the investor does not have much to lose. But as you know, bear markets can rise up at the most inopportune times. The closer you are to retirement, the more difficult it will be to recover from a bear market.

Consider the following example: You invest $5,000 a year, earning 11.3 percent annually for twenty years. With no bear markets to interrupt the growth of your investment, your $100,000 would grow to $369,826. That's the good news. Let's see what happens if a bear market equivalent to the 1973-74 or 2000-02 declines hit early in the life of your dollar cost averaging plan, such as the first year. Your $100,000 would still grow to $348,456 after twenty years. Not bad. That is because you still had plenty of time to recover from your early loss, and your loss was only on the first $5,000 invested.

Now, take a bear market of the same magnitude in the twentieth year of your investment program, maybe just as you were about to retire. Oops! The value drops to $184,082 because the 44.6 percent drop affects all the money you have accumulated over twenty years, not just the first $5,000. Investing another $5,000 under dollar cost averaging is not going to make up for that $185,000 loss. That's the bad news. See Chart 7-1.

If you want to use dollar cost averaging to build up your portfolio in your early years, go ahead; but keep in mind that with each passing year the amount at risk increases, and your time left to recoup your losses decreases! A person with an established portfolio at or near retirement age must avoid the big losses from which he or she can never recover. That's where a proven active risk management strategy can be crucial. Active risk management provides the potential to grow your financial nest egg through stock market advances while hopefully keeping bear market losses to acceptable levels, preserving valuable capital and safeguarding your retirement funds. Remember, dollar cost averaging combined with active risk management can be a dynamite combination; but dollar cost averaging alone may blow up in your face.

## Chart 7-1

### Dollar Cost Averaging
### $5,000/Year for 20 Years

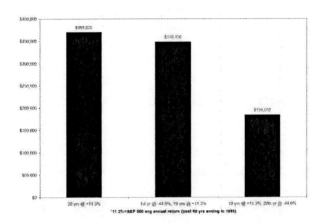

*Courtesy of SIMCO*

## Key Points to Remember:

- As another form of the buy and hold strategy, dollar cost averaging leaves your portfolio open to significant erosion in the face of a bear market.
- If you want to use dollar cost averaging to build up your portfolio in your early years, go ahead; but keep in mind that with each passing year the amount at risk increases, and your time left to recoup your losses decreases.
- Dollar cost averaging combined with active risk management can be a dynamite combination; but dollar cost averaging alone may blow up in your face.

# MYTH #8

## The stock market is a random walk. No one can predict what it is going to do.

"When the longer term, which has been all but ignored by random walk theorists, is viewed in the light of market forecasting indicators, it becomes clear that the market does not follow a random pattern, and that superior profits await investors willing to follow the guidance of those indicators!"

—*Norman G. Fosback*
*Stock Market Logic*

### Random Walk Hogwash

There are many competing theories of how Wall Street really works. Some investors subscribe to the Efficient Market Theory that the market instantly incorporates all available information into stock prices. Other investors believe in the Random Walk Theory that the stock market follows no rhyme or reason. Actually, Random Walk is a version of the Efficient Market Theory. As Edgar Peters says in *Chaos and Order in the Capital Markets*, "Market efficiency does not necessarily imply a random walk, but a random walk does imply market efficiency."

Nonetheless, it is generally the Random Walk version that is being referred to when the term Efficient Market Theory is used.

CNBC's Ron Insana hits the nail on the head in his book, *Traders' Tales*. "There is only one certainty about academic studies of Wall Street . . . most ivory tower professors haven't a clue as to how the stock market really works." Dr. Joe Kiely, a professor of finance at several major universities and now President of Kiely Financial Services in Greenville, North Carolina, echoed Insana when he stated, "I grew up on the academic side, but you guys on the active investment management side are the ones that get it."

There are always plenty of naysayers. For years, the experts said that humans could never run a four minute mile. Roger Bannister proved the skeptics wrong. Once Bannister broke the barrier, the four-minute mile became commonplace.

In an interview, Peter Lynch summed up Random Walk as hogwash. " . . . Wharton professors who believed in it weren't doing nearly as well as my colleagues at Fidelity. If you believe in Random Walk, you have to believe my Fidelity colleagues' and my success was a fluke. It's hard to support a theory that says the market is irrational when you know somebody who just made a 20-fold profit in Kentucky Fried Chicken and explained in advance why it was going to rise."

Ironically enough, two finance professors agree with Peter Lynch. In their book, *A Non-Random Walk Down Wall Street*, Andrew W. Lo from MIT and A. Craig MacKinlay from the Wharton School of Business at the University of Pennsylvania put the Random Walk Theory to the test—and it failed! "Our research findings have several implications for financial economists and investors. The fact that the Random Walk Theory can be rejected for recent U.S. equity returns suggests the presence of predictable components in the stock market. This opens the door to superior long-term investment returns through disciplined active investment management."

Demonstrating that stock market moves are indeed predictable, Jeremy J. Siegel reported in his book, *Stocks for the Long Run*, the results of studying the 200-day moving average of stock prices for over 100 years (from 1885 through 1993). He used a one percent band around the 200-day moving average to prevent an investor from getting whipsawed with frequent moves in and out of the market. Using the 200-day moving average, an investor is in stocks during all the important bull markets and out of stocks during all the major bear markets. Over the whole period, this simple 200-day moving average market timing strategy earned an excess return of 1.52 percent per year over a buy and hold strategy. Most significantly, it allowed the investor to miss the Great Crash in 1929. Siegel concluded that while the 200-day moving average strategy does not raise overall returns dramatically, it does substantially lower risk.

Siegel and others have shown that simple market timing methods can and do reduce risk and deserve a good, hard look. I take that one step further and contend that most active risk management professionals employ much more sophisticated market timing models than a simple moving average, with the potential to deliver reduced risk plus superior risk-adjusted returns.

Peter Lynch is right, Random Walk is pure hogwash, and we have the research and actual investment results to prove it. Look at the data in Chart 8-

1 provided by Select Advisors (www.select-advisors.com), the active managers network. Roger Schreiner and his team at Select Advisors have put together a program that tracks active management investment advisors and makes data about their actual performance available to investors through a proprietary wrap fee program. Look at Chart 8-1 below for the Select Advisors Top 10 versus the S&P 500 and the NASDAQ Composite. I believe that you will have to agree that this did not happen by accident. In Myth #19, we will address the issue of how to give an investor the best chance of identifying and utilizing the managers and strategies that will do the best in the future.

## Chart 8-1

### Select Advisors Statistics Averages, Top 10

|          | Return  | S&P    | NASDAQ  |
|----------|---------|--------|---------|
| 3 Month  | 29.40%  | -12.18 | -14.53  |
| 6 Month  | 57.69%  | -24.9  | -33.03  |
| 12 Month | 53.69%  | -16.07 | -16.37  |
| 24 Month | 51.97%  | -40.1  | -66.89  |
| QTD      | 31.52%  | -13.63 | -16.51  |
| YTD      | 67.17%  | -25.53 | -37.37  |

*As of 9/26/2002*
*Return=percentage return over the period*
*S&P=Standard and Poors 500 Index*
*NASDAQ=NASDAQ Composite Index*
*Courtesy of Select Advisors*

"Why would there be structure in financial markets? Why should the data cluster in predictable
patterns? The short answer is simple: financial
markets are the product of human activity, and
human beings are trend-following, herd-driven crea-
tures, who react and overreact en masse. I believe
in the *in*efficient-market theory, based on human
foibles and the herd behavior of people acting in
groups."

—*Doyne Farmer*
*Prediction Corporation*
*Santa Fe, New Mexico*

## Key Points to Remember:

- The stock market is *not* a random walk.
- Through disciplined active investment management, stock market moves are predictable
  enough to produce superior risk-adjusted
  returns over the long term.

# MYTH #9

## Asset allocation reduces risk *and* increases returns.

"Over the years, we have heard all the clichés about investment strategy, such as asset allocation, diversification, buy and hold, etc. We now know that asset allocation (how your assets are divided among equities, bonds, and cash) is not a risk-reduction strategy or even a return-enhancement approach. It has failed abysmally in all of these areas since it was first touted."

—*Jerry White*
*CSA News Magazine*

When Jerry White, a writer for *CSA News Magazine*, a Canadian senior citizens publication, states that the traditional passive asset allocation investment approach is not even a risk reduction strategy much less a return enhancement approach, he may be overstating his case. The point he is trying to make is that in times of crisis, we have seen all asset classes (except cash), go down in value; thus his conclusion that passive asset allocation has been a failure. Let me review the basics of asset allocation and put his statement as well as this myth in the proper perspective.

## Asset Allocation Basics

Taking a close look at asset allocation sets the stage for a review of active risk management. Asset allocation is an investment strategy aimed at reducing risk and enhancing investment return by investing in a variety of asset types with infrequent changes in the allocation mix.

The theory behind asset allocation lies in attempting to invest in a sufficiently diversified asset universe with an optimal mix to achieve the desired return or some increment above it, with reduced risk. Periodic rebalancing helps eliminate the risk of the portfolio becoming too concentrated in any one asset class and exposing the portfolio to sharp value declines due to a change in the economic climate. Critics of asset allocation will say that the classic 60 percent stocks, 30 percent bonds, 10 percent cash allocation mix still exposes a portfolio to too much risk in a bear market like we had from March 2000 to October 2002. After all, 60 percent of a 50 percent decline is still a 30 percent loss in account value.

A major benefit of asset allocation is that it removes the emotional aspect from investment decision-making, allowing investors to make a long-term commitment to a specific investment strategy. Another benefit of employing asset allocation is the ability to diversify your assets to guard against poor performance in one asset category devastating your portfolio. The theory is that as one asset class in the portfolio underperforms due to changing economic and market conditions, other classes negatively correlated with that asset class compensate for that declining performance with rising returns. For example, during inflationary times, total returns on fixed income investments such as long-term government bonds typically decline while total returns on hard assets such as precious metals increase.

Therefore, it is crucial that the optimum mix include asset classes that move in opposite directions to each other (i.e. are non-correlated). Combinations of asset classes with low or negative correlations help to reduce risk. Once the acceptable level of risk is determined, the optimum combination of asset classes is created to hopefully provide the greatest level of return possible without exceeding the predetermined level of acceptable risk.

While the classic passive asset allocation strategy described above can reduce risk, it also reduces potential return compared to the performance of the top individual investment classes in the portfolio. Further, it ignores the fact that during a deflationary period or in other times of crisis, all asset classes (except cash) may go down in value. In order to maintain a reduced risk posture plus enhance portfolio returns, investment managers have turned to dynamic asset allocation or what we have been calling active risk management.

David B. Loeper of financeware.com sums up the Asset Allocation Myth as follows. "The theory behind asset allocation is based on some simple premises. The core theory is that by blending two or more assets that do not move in lock step (non-correlated), one can improve their return per unit of risk. Much of the theory dates back to work done long ago by Bill Sharpe and Harry Markowitz. Their work, now widely accepted and some of it Nobel Prize winning, has become the 'Investing 101' of investment management."

"Sometimes, however, theories fail in practice. That is the case with asset allocation. Many practitioners (including Sharpe himself) have given up on the basic asset allocation theory and the 'optimized' portfolios that go with it. For the theoretical portfolio that is free from the realities of contributions, withdrawals, taxes, dividends or interest, asset allocation is Nobel Prize winning work. For the rest of us that have to deal with these realities, it may actually cause more harm than good."

## Getting Dynamic

The dynamic asset allocation strategy involves continuous monitoring and rebalancing of the portfolio among multiple asset classes. While the rebalancing under classic passive asset allocation (or strategic asset allocation) returns the portfolio to predetermined asset mix ranges, dynamic asset allocation analyzes the performance for each class or fund and adjusts the portfolio mix in an attempt to select and/or weight investment classes or funds with the greatest potential for superior returns in the current economic environment. Thus the allocation of assets takes on a dynamic nature . . . changing in response to market conditions and anticipated opportunities for investment gain. The rebalancing usually takes place in increments.

Jerry Wagner of Flexible Plan Investments, Ltd.* (1-800-347-3539, www.flexibleplan.com) has been one of the most successful practicioners of dynamic asset allocation with his Evolution™ investment process. Evolution™ has been hypothetically tested back to 1973 and has been used in the management of actual accounts since 1996. Chart 9-1 below shows the actual results for Evolution™ accounts from 1996 through 2001. It is rare that you get the opportunity to evaluate an investment strategy over both a bull and bear market period this early in a product cycle.

It appears that Flexible Plan's Evolution™ has passed its initial test with flying colors. Of course, past performance is no guarantee of future returns.

## Chart 9-1

### Evolution™ (After Max Fees)

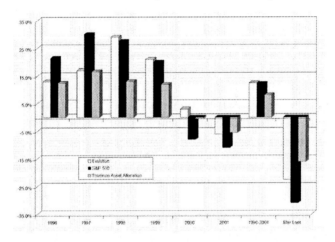

*Source: S&P 500 Composite Total Return, Thomson and Average Evolution™ Returns from FPI Model Accounts. Summary after 1.8% annual fee, deducted quarterly.*
*Courtesy of Flexible Plan Investments, Ltd.*
*See Appendix B for Disclosure Statement*

*\* New SIMCO, Inc., a wholly owned subsidiary of Flexible Plan Investments, Ltd., purchased the investment advisory assets of SIMCO, a Texas corporation wholly owned by John Sosnowy, on March 31, 2001. Mr. Sosnowy remains President of SIMCO and is a Vice-President and Portfolio Manager of Flexible Plan Investments, Ltd.*

Economic realities make dynamic asset allocation a realistic strategy. First, financial markets tend to move in cycles. It only makes good economic sense to try to capitalize on the upside potential of asset classes or funds poised to outperform less vibrant or declining asset classes or funds via a shift in weighting within the portfolio mix.

Second, investing in the right sector of the market at the right time can produce superior investment returns. It is not uncommon for top performing sectors to turn in annual returns of 50 percent or more. While the downside potential of some market sectors makes investing in these areas potentially dangerous in a fixed or static asset allocation strategy, dynamic asset allocation takes advantage of the unique opportunity to move in and out of these sectors as economic conditions dictate. As a result, investment returns can significantly outpace the overall market and fixed asset allocation strategies.

Third, participating in superior returns within established risk parameters means that the dynamic asset allocator does not have to be right 100 percent of the time. The key is to be right enough times over a full market cycle to deliver superior returns on a risk-adjusted basis. If you achieve this, you will outpace the impact of inflation and taxes and achieve real investment growth to add to your retirement nest egg.

Fourth, bear markets are a fact of life in financial markets and investing. If implemented properly, dynamic asset allocation should reduce exposure to declining markets and a devastating bear attack on portfolio value. The more capital investors lose on the downside, the longer it takes to recapture their losses. Likewise, the more money lost, the less available to capitalize on opportunities when the market moves higher. A review of bear markets shows that investors have spent 76 percent of their time suffering through bear markets and trying to recoup their losses to get back to breakeven. Less than a fourth of their time was actually spent increasing the value of their original investment. These facts are validated in an article entitled "Why Market Timing Works" by Jerry Wagner in the Summer 1997 issue of *The Journal of Investing*. See Chart 9-2 for a recap of the impact of various bear markets since September 1929.

## Chart 9-2

S&P 500 INDEX BEAR MARKET STUDY
September 1929 through June 2002

| Bear Market | Duration | % Decline | Time Needed To Breakeven |
|---|---|---|---|
| Sept. '29—June '32 | 33 months | 86.7 | 25.2 years |
| July '33—Mar. '35 | 20 months | 33.9 | 2.3 years |
| Mar. '37—Mar. '38 | 12 months | 54.5 | 8.8 years |
| Nov. '38—Apr. '42 | 41 months | 45.8 | 6.4 years |
| May '46—Mar. '48 | 22 months | 28.1 | 4.1 years |
| Aug. '56—Oct. '57 | 14 months | 21.6 | 2.1 years |
| Dec. '61—June '62 | 6 months | 28 | 1.8 years |
| Feb. '66—Oct. '66 | 8 months | 22.2 | 1.4 years |
| Nov. '68—May '70 | 18 months | 36.1 | 3.3 years |
| Jan. '73—Oct. '74 | 21 months | 48.2 | 7.6 years |
| Nov. '80—Aug. '82 | 21 months | 27.1 | 2.1 years |
| Aug. '87—Dec. '87 | 21 months | 27.1 | 2.1 years |
| July '90—Oct. '90 | 4 months | 33.5 | 1.9 years |
| Mar. '00—Oct. '02 | 31 months | 49.2 | N/A |

*Courtesy of Fabian Investor Resource*

Of course, no investment system is perfect. The success of dynamic asset allocation rests on the ability of the investment professional to properly identify those asset classes or funds poised to deliver the highest returns in each market phase. Remem-

ber, you don't have to be right 100 percent of the
time.

## Tapping Technology

Without a doubt, we live in an age of technology.
Many facets of dynamic asset allocation, active risk
management, and market timing would not exist without the state-of-the-art computers, software, and online
databases available today. Savvy investment managers have at their fingertips powerful analysis tools for
studying the market and developing complex dynamic
asset allocation and timing models. Using models back-
tested against historical data, investment managers
have created criteria and models which indicate which
asset class or classes are positioned to outperform
other asset classes in the current market environment.

**"Starting with the basic signal, we will add new
features, building on the model progressively. At each
stage of development, we test for curve-fitting. What
finally emerges is a profitable stock market timing
model that is also robust."**

*—Nelson Freeburg*
*Formula Research*

Assuming a working knowledge of the market and
economic cycles, investment advisors can track a range
of indicators to determine a number of factors such as
data patterns which signal a fundamental change in
the economic climate, what people are doing in the
market, and the relative attractiveness of specific asset classes or funds. Armed with this information, the
investment manager develops an asset allocation strategy which apportions monies among the portfolio's dif-

ferent asset classes or funds based on return probabilities and portfolio risk parameters.

While fixed asset allocation keeps you locked into asset classes which are exhibiting signs of decline or which are unlikely to show much return in the near-term, the use of technology opens up new horizons for detecting market moves and the expected relative returns from specific asset classes or funds in the current or anticipated environment. The adept money manager, using dynamic asset allocation techniques, has the potential to move in and out of investments to take advantage of superior return opportunities and sidestep the worst of devastating bear market moves.

A private research study by Barra/Micropal released in William E. Donoghue's *Moneyletter*, found that Peter Lynch's success during his years at the helm of the Fidelity Magellan Fund was grounded in the fund's asset allocation. When biotechnology stocks were on the upswing, those stocks were the most heavily represented in the Magellan portfolio. When blue chips outpaced the market as a whole, blue chip stocks dominated the portfolio.

Dynamic asset allocation delivers the following distinct investment advantages:

- Diversification among a number of asset classes reduces risk and increases the probability that an investor will be invested in the top performing asset classes when they are making their upside moves.
- Changing the weights or allocation ratios allows an investor to take greater advantage of top performing segments of the market.
- Adjusting the allocation in response to market trends can mean the likelihood of less loss when the value of an asset class tumbles.
- Adopting a disciplined dynamic asset alloca-

tion strategy eliminates the emotional factor
that can trigger poor investment decisions.

**"The stock market has a history of moving to ir-
rational extremes because, on a short-term basis,
stock prices are often more a reflection of fear, greed,
or other psychological factors than of business and
monetary fundamentals."**

*—Joseph L. Oppenheimer*

Dynamic asset allocation strategies do not always
outperform the broad market. However, as a general
rule, they do reduce losses during down markets, preserving portfolio value and safeguarding assets to be
redeployed during upside moves. Overall, they are designed to outperform buy and hold strategies on a risk-
adjusted basis and often outperform buy and hold strategies on a total return basis.

To clear up any confusion over buy and hold, passive asset allocation, and dynamic asset allocation,
consider the following distinctions. Some people con-
fuse a buy and hold strategy with passive asset allocation. The buy and hold investor purchases securities and hangs on to them for the long haul despite
changes in market conditions. The passive asset allocation investor periodically rebalances the portfolio
because market action causes it to stray from predetermined targets or ranges for asset classes. Asset
classes experiencing strong market performance become overweighted relative to their target, and portfolio maintenance requires bringing them back in line
with the original targets, for example; 60 percent stocks,
30 percent bonds, and 10 percent cash.

Think of it this way. When an investment manager
periodically rebalances back to the target, it is consid-

ered passive asset allocation. Adding a new dimension, dynamic asset allocation adjusts the portfolio mix in reaction to changes in asset class or fund relative strength or market conditions. If the investment manager evaluates current economic conditions and chooses to depart from the strategic mix in order to take advantage of market or fund opportunities, that is dynamic asset allocation. The investment manager is attempting to adjust the portfolio mix based on relative undervaluations and overvaluations in order to capitalize on opportunities as market dynamics change over time.

**"You do have to know what time of market it is. Markets go in cycles like all the other rhythms of life."**

*—Adam Smith*
*The Money Game*

## Key Points to Remember:

- Asset allocation can reduce risk, but asset allocation strategies can reduce return, too!
- Simple passive asset allocation probably will not save you from significant losses during a bear market.
- The dynamic asset allocation strategy involves continuous monitoring and rebalancing of the portfolio among multiple asset classes.
- If implemented properly, dynamic asset allocation should reduce exposure to declining markets and a devastating bear attack on portfolio value, and give you the potential for superior risk-adjusted returns.

# MYTH #10

## Invest in what you know or where you work.

"The 'invest in what you know' approach is at least partly responsible for the fact that employees typically allocate more than a third of their retirement account assets to the stock of the company for which they work, despite the risks of such a strategy: your biggest investment—your job—is already tied to the fortunes of your workplace, so by stashing retirement assets in your company stock, you're putting too many eggs in one basket. That's why most financial planning pros recommend you keep no more than 10 percent of your 401(k) assets in your own company's shares."

*—Gary Belsky and Thomas Gilovich*
*Why Smart People Make Big Money Mistakes*

As I have said earlier, diversification among a number of asset classes reduces risk and increases the potential that an investor will be at least partially invested in the top performing asset classes when they are making their upside moves. Diversification is the spreading of investment risk by owning different types of securities, investments in different geographical markets, etc. (i.e. not putting all of your eggs in one basket, one company, or even one industry).

If you are an employee of a major corporation with a 401(k) plan, the chances are good that the majority, if not all, of your portfolio is concentrated in one stock. Not only that, but your day-to-day income comes from that same company, and your 401(k) contributions may be concentrated in that same stock, too! While the company is doing well and we are in the throes of a bull market, that is great. However, when the market trends change, as they have since 2000, your nest egg will be at risk; and if the economy retreats enough, even your job could be in jeopardy.

Look at the stars of the post-WWII bull market, the so-called "Nifty Fifty" of the late 60's and early 70's. The "religion stocks" or "one-decision stocks" in that group included IBM, Xerox, and Polaroid. In the bull market of the 1990's, many investors leaped to the conclusion that you could outperform the market if you simply held onto its biggest and best companies, names such as Enron, WorldCom, or Global Crossing. Today we know that that was not too smart. Not only did those stocks go down dramatically, but history from the 1970's shows that they do not necessarily come back strong either.

In the 1973-74 bear market, Polaroid, for example, traded at 97 times earnings near the high, and then dropped from $126 down to less than $19, a decline of 85 percent in value. It did not move above its December 1972 high until 1999—almost 27 years later. How would you have liked to have had all your eggs in that basket?

Second, a portfolio invested equally in 1972's favorite growth stocks sharply lagged the S&P 500 from the end of 1972 to the fall of 2002. According to

*InvesTech Research*, a $25,000 portfolio with dividends reinvested would have increased to $467,997 for an 11.8 percent annual gain, while the same investment in the S&P 500 would have resulted in a portfolio worth $712,243, a 13.6 percent annual gain.

Therefore, diversification is one key to protecting your nest egg. Diversification allows you to hedge against declines in one particular stock or industry. Think of it as an "investment firewall." It does not mean that a hacker still won't get through or that a market decline will not occur, it just helps to reduce the probabilities of your computer being totally wiped out, or having all of your eggs in a basket like Polaroid of 1972, the can't miss "New Era" company that made investors zero return for the next 27 years, or Enron in 2001.

There is also a good lesson about diversification to be learned from the oil industry of the 70's and 80's—Boomtown, USA. Oil prices were sky high and rising. It seemed like almost everyone associated with the industry was striking it rich, no matter whether they were in drilling, speculating, or prospecting. In addition to all of the people working in the industry, millions more were investing in oil stocks and/or drilling funds. At this time, it became commonplace, though foolish, to think of diversification as owning ten different oil stocks. And, of course, there were many people that both worked and invested in the industry. The boom continued for over 10 years; but by the mid 80's, the OPEC cartel fell apart, oil prices crashed, and many people lost everything—their jobs, their investment portfolios, and their retirement savings. As you undoubtedly are aware, this costly pattern was repeated in the 1990's with technology stocks.

Reasons to diversify:

- Hedge against a decline in one stock
- Hedge against a decline in one industry

True diversification (or asset allocation) is between non-correlated or low market correlation assets. Otherwise, it is of little value. So to take your high-tech windfall from one company and invest in ten different high-tech startups is not real diversification. And even true diversification may not be enough.

Now repeat after me: No stock is bulletproof. Not Microsoft. Not GE. Not Big Blue. Not Ma Bell. Not [your company here]. Some are less vulnerable, but shifting consumer tastes and new technologies can devastate any company, any time.

Meanwhile, there are steps you can take. For starters, do not buy more company stock if you're getting a healthy slug of it from the boss. If you exercise stock options, diversify immediately. Remember, your most valuable asset—your career—is also tied to the health of your firm. If you're over age 55, your employer may allow you to sell some of its stock held in your 401(k), so be sure to ask. In your taxable account, lean toward diversified mutual funds, or individual stocks in at least six industries—and avoid the one in which you work. If you are concentrated in a single stock in a taxable account, you will have to pay capital-gains tax as you diversify. In most cases, that's a price worth paying.

## Key Points to Remember:

- If the majority of your portfolio is concentrated in your company's stock, when the market trends change, your nest egg will be

at risk; and if the economy retreats enough,
your job could be in jeopardy as well.

· Diversification is one key to protecting your
  nest egg.
· Diversification allows you to hedge against
  declines in one particular stock or industry.
· No stock is bulletproof.

# MYTH #11

## Time in the market, not market timing, is the key to investment success.

"It's ironic that people question market timing, but accept stock picking. If you believe that someone can pick stocks and beat the market, why can't they time the market? In the long run, it's easier to time the market than to pick stocks!"

*—Marty Zweig, PhD.*

### Missing the Up Days Doesn't Really Matter . . . If You Also Miss The Down Days

One predictable result of a down market is a rash of articles extolling investors to stay fully invested and not to try to practice disciplined risk management or to try to time the market because they are doomed to failure. After all, what if you miss some of those very good days because you are out of the market? And, of course, the answer is that your returns would be greatly diminished.

You might even buy this argument . . . until you look at the other side of the coin . . . what happens if you miss the worst days with your risk management strategy, which is, of course, your objective? Now the potential payoff of timing the market shines as performance soars (See Chart 11-1).

Actually, both of these arguments have very little statistical validity. The odds of missing only the best or only the worst days of the market are virtually nil because the best and worst days often occur back-to-back. If you miss one, you'll probably also miss the other. So the real question should be . . . what happens if you miss both the best and the worst days? The answer is that the raw numbers show that an investor would actually exceed buy and hold performance and achieve a relatively stable return if both the best *and* worst 10, 20, 30 or 40 days were missed.

## Chart 11-1: April 1984—May 2000

| If you missed just the BEST: | Your return FELL to: |
|---|---|
| 10 days | 11.59% |
| 20 days | 9.40% |
| 30 days | 7.51% |
| 40 days | 5.77% |
| | |
| If you missed just the WORST: | Your return ROSE to: |
| 10 days | 20.89% |
| 20 days | 23.68% |
| 30 days | 25.99% |
| 40 days | 28.13% |
| | |
| If you missed both the BEST and WORST: | Your return was: |
| 10 days | 17.29% |
| 20 days | 17.78% |
| 30 days | 17.63% |
| 40 days | 17.83% |

*Courtesy of Warwick Investment Management, Inc.*

As a point of reference, the buy and hold annual return for the S&P 500 during the same time period was 15.02 percent. Naturally, we need to point out that the S&P 500 is an index, and you could not have invested directly in the S&P 500 to achieve these results. However, there are a number of index funds that have proven to track the S&P 500 very closely, making this a realistic example.

Part of the reason for the benefits of missing both the best and worst days is that the worst days are often far worse than the best days. Plus, there's the impact of the mathematics of gains and losses. If you lose 20 percent you have to achieve a 25 percent gain to return to breakeven. A 50 percent loss requires a 100 percent gain to return to breakeven. In Chart 11-2 showing the 10 worst and 10 best days for the S&P 500 from April 1984 to September 2002, cumulative losses from just 10 bad days come to— 55.21 percent. Recouping just those 10 days of losses will take a +123.26 percent return, but the 10 best days only produced +70.45 percent.

# Chart 11-2: April 1984-September 2002

| The 10 WORST DOWN Days | PERCENT LOSS | The 10 BEST UP Days | PERCENT GAIN |
|---|---|---|---|
| Sept. 11, 1986 | -4.81% | | |
| Oct. 16, 1987 | -5.16% | | |
| Oct. 19, 1987 | -20.47% | | |
| | | Oct. 20, 1987 | 5.33% |
| | | Oct. 21, 1987 | 9.10% |
| Oct. 26, 1987 | -8.28% | | |
| | | Oct. 29, 1987 | 4.93% |
| Jan. 8, 1988 | -6.77% | | |
| Oct. 13, 1989 | -6.12% | | |
| Oct. 27, 1997 | -6.87% | | |
| | | Oct. 28, 1997 | 5.12% |
| Aug. 31, 1998 | -6.80% | | |
| | | Sept. 8, 1998 | 5.09% |
| | | Mar. 16, 2000 | 4.76% |
| Apr. 14, 2000 | -5.83% | | |
| | | Jan. 3, 2001 | 5.01% |
| | | April 5, 2001 | 4.37% |
| Sept. 17, 2001 | -4.92% | | |
| | | July 24, 2002 | 5.73% |
| | | July 29, 2002 | 5.41% |
| | -55.21% | | 70.45% |

*Courtesy of SIMCO*

Making these statistics even more interesting is the historical pattern of best and worst days. Genuinely bad days in the market rarely happen in isolation. There is typically a pattern of nervousness in the market, a series of small losses that may be accelerating until suddenly investors as a whole turn skittish, pushing the market down to a bigger loss. As you can see from the chart above, many of the best one-day returns occur shortly after a major decline. For example, look at 1997. The worst down day ever in terms of Dow points took place on October 27th with a downside move of 554 points. The very next day, October 28th, was the best up day ever with an upside rebound of 337 points. If you missed one, you probably missed both.

In order to be successful, risk management market timing does not have to be perfect. Despite belief to the contrary, market timing does not target getting in and out of the market at the absolute bottoms and tops. It does, however, strive to get an investor's funds out of the market before a major bear market devastates the portfolio. The first and foremost priority of an active risk management (or market timing) strategy is the preservation of capital.

A University of Michigan study on the effect of daily and monthly market swings on a portfolio's performance came up with an interesting statistic on active risk management. Based on monthly data . . . "the perfect timer would have turned a $1 investment in January 1926 into $690 million in December 1993. In comparison, a $1 investment in the market index would have grown to $637.30 while $1 invested in Treasury bills would have grown to $9.20."

To be sure, there is no such thing as a perfect market timing (or any other investment) strategy. However, the University of Michigan study dramatically illustrates the value of missing the worst days of the market. With a nearly $689 million margin for error over the 68-year period, market timing does not have to be perfect to produce superior risk-adjusted returns over a full market cycle of both bull and bear market moves.

By exiting the market before the onset of the major portion of the bear market, this strategy has the potential to preserve capital for those subsequent bull market periods and can position an investor to participate in the bulk of the upside swing with a majority of his or her investment funds intact.

As we saw previously in Chart 9-2, on average, a bear market has reared its ugly head about every five years since 1929. The average duration of a bear market has been approximately nineteen months. Equally important, it has taken an average three and one half years to make up the loss suffered during a bear market.

Why allow bear markets to eat up your hard earned investment gains and spend the majority of your time recouping losses suffered during a bear market? It simply does not make good economic sense. Yet that is exactly what buy and hold proponents suggest you do.

When academicians say "market timing does not work," I firmly believe what they are really saying is, "I can't make it work," or "I don't understand how it works." Well, I really don't understand how electricity powers things or why airplanes fly, but I don't go around making a fool of myself saying that they don't work!

Bob Carver's long-term research, whose results appeared in the May 2002 issue of *Investment Advisor* magazine, is an enlightening study which suggests that market timing might not be so bad after all. According to Carver, there are long periods in history when the market moves higher on a trend basis, but there are also periods when the market churns sideways, with large percentage declines and advances. This tends to lead to long-term investor frustration and disappointment with buy and hold strategies. It's almost inevitable that the majority of investors will give up on the stock market during severe declines such as we had from 2000 to 2002.

Often, those investors are too traumatized by the experience to reenter those stock positions for the advance that inevitably has followed.

With the very strong uptrend of the 80's and 90's behind us, Carver performed a long-term regression study of the S&P 500. The results of that study tell us that even after the last few years of bear market decline, the index is still more than 50 percent above its median price trend as measured from the 1932 low to the present. That's not to suggest the market will inevitably return to its median trend anytime soon, but it could mean that the downside risk has yet to be wrung completely out of the market.

The study also suggests that the market is very likely to spend a considerable amount of time going sideways, with substantial intermediate-term dips and rallies creating an ideal situation for skillful active risk managers.

In Myth #4, we met Connie Conservative. She tried to play it safe by investing only in Treasury Bills and government bonds but ended up flat broke. Well, now I'd like to introduce you to two other investors that used different investment strategies.

Peter Hope (a fictional character, though his situation is not) began a buy and hold investment strategy upon his retirement in 1973. He invested $50,000 in a diversified stock portfolio and $50,000 in an aggressive growth stock mutual fund, and set up a systematic withdrawal plan of $8,000 annually (adjusted for inflation) just like Connie Conservative. He held on hoping that a bear market would not come along during his retirement years and devour his money. Unfortunately, a big bad bear market lurked right around the corner, rearing its ugly head in 1973 and 1974.

The one/two punch of market depreciation of his

portfolios and increased withdrawals due to inflation wiped out his aggressive growth stock fund entirely by 1978. His diversified stock portfolio suffered the same fate, declining to a zero balance by
1984. Peter was last sighted in a soup kitchen line
and resides nearby under a freeway underpass.

| Peter Hope | |
|---|---|
| Amount Invested: | $100,000 |
| Total Amount Withdrawn through 12/31/1984: | $102,773 |
| Portfolio Value As of 12/31/1984: | $—0— |
| Financial Status: | Destitute |

Meanwhile, Sammy Savvy (a fictional character,
though his situation is not), who retired at the same
time with the same investment and regular withdrawal plan, hired a risk manager (active risk manager or market timer) to monitor his portfolio on a
daily basis and to protect him from the full consequences of debilitating bear markets. It made all the
difference in the world. When we caught up with
Sammy's wife on the beach in Hawaii, her tan and
sunny disposition exuded success.

She said Sammy died a happy and wealthy man
on New Year's Eve, 1995. After searching through
his records, she told us that at the time of his death,
Sammy's annual withdrawal to supplement Social
Security and other retirement income totaled over
$30,000 compared with the initial $8,000. More importantly, his original $100,000 investment had
grown to in excess of $1.3 million, despite withdraw-
als exceeding $450,000 over the years and paying
his advisory fees for active risk management.

| Sammy Savvy | |
| --- | --- |
| Amount Invested: | $100,000 |
| Total Amount Withdrawn through 12/31/1995: | $450,800 |
| Portfolio Value As of 12/31/1995: | $1,308,533 |
| Financial Status: Independently Wealthy | |

Employing a buy and hold, more appropriately called a buy and hope, strategy with a diversifed stock portfolio has not proved to be the answer. You are just hoping that a prolonged bear market does not strike.

Psychologists have discovered two important facts about investors. First, the primary emotions that determine risk-taking behavior are not greed and fear, but *hope* and fear, as psychologist Lola Lopes pointed out in 1987. Second, although to err is human indeed, financial practitioners of all types, from portfolio managers to corporate executives, make the same mistakes repeatedly.

The real answer lies in reducing your risk exposure!

Paul Merriman said back in the 1990's when the bull market was still raging: "The idea that everybody is going to buy and hold is outrageous. The question is, do you want market risk management or not? Mutual funds do not give that to you. After we have a huge bear market, people will say, Boy, that market timing is a great idea." Well, that was certainly prophetic. There was an article in *USA Today* just the other day, after the stock market had been savaged for 2 ½ years, finally touting the virtues of market timing as a risk management strategy. It was about time.

## The Rest of the Story

One of the common criticisms of risk management strategies is the possibility of missing some of the gains in bull markets and not avoiding all the losses in bear markets. While the criticism has some validity, there is more to the story.

A review of the big quarterly buy and hold gains and losses (gains of more than 5 percent and losses exceeding 3 percent) compared with the results for the same quarters of risk management using one timing model used in actual accounts since 1970 sheds some interesting light.

In Chart 11-3, note that the risk management results averaged 3.2 percent less than the buy and hold strategy in the highly profitable quarters. That's to be expected. On the other hand, the risk management strategy results outperformed the buy and hold investment approach by an average 8.4 percent in the worst losing quarters.

# Chart 11-3

### COMPARISON OF "BUY AND HOLD" VS. "THE TIMING MODEL" 01/01/1970 to 12/31/2001 NYSE Index

| | |
|---|---|
| # of Highly Profitable Quarters Buy and Hold (Gains >5%) | 61 |
| Average Profit per Highly Profitable Quarter Buy and Hold | 11.80% |
| Average Same Quarter Profit with The Timing Model | 8.60% |
| Advantage with Buy and Hold | 3.20% |
| | |
| # of Very Unprofitable Quarters Buy and Hold (Losses >3%) | 27 |
| Average Loss per Very Unprofitable Quarter Buy and Hold | -10.90% |
| Average Same Quarter Results with The Timing Model | -2.50% |
| Advantage with The Timing Model | 8.40% |

*Courtesy of SIMCO*
*NYSE=New York Stock Exchange Total Return Index*
*See Appendix C for Disclosure Statement*

Conclusion: Active risk management market timing has historically accomplished its goal of reducing losses in the worst markets and nearly matching the big gain performances of buy and hold strategies in the best markets.

## Key Points to Remember:

- Market timing, not time in the market, is the key to investment success.
- The odds of missing only the best or only the worst days of the market with an active strategy are virtually nil because the best and worst days often occur back-to-back.
- Employing a buy and hold, more appropriately called a buy and hope, strategy with a diversified stock portfolio is not the answer. You are just hoping that a prolonged bear market does not strike.
- Risk management market timing has historically accomplished its goal of reducing losses in the worst markets and nearly matching the big gain performances of buy and hold strategies in the best markets.

# MYTH #12

## Market timing is a relatively new investment strategy without proven results.

"Quite often, when someone says something won't work, what they really mean is, 'I can't make it work!'"

*—John K. Sosnowy*
*SAAFTI Conference, May 1996*

There are successful active practitioners of market timing today with thirty to forty years of experience. For those who say market timing will never work, let them ponder these other famous prophesies from the past:

"Radio has no future."
"X-rays will prove to be a hoax."
"Heavier-than-air flying machines are impossible."
   —William Thomson, Lord Kelvin
   English scientist (1824-1907)

"Who the hell wants to hear actors talk?"
   —Harry M. Warner
   Founder, Warner Bros. Studio (1927)

"Rail travel at high speeds is not possible because passengers, unable to breathe, would die of asphyxia."
—Dionysius Lardner
English scientist (1793-1859)

"While theoretically and technically television may be feasible, commercially and financially I consider it an impossibility . . . . "
—Lee DeForest
American inventor (1873-1961)

For those looking for proven results, let's look at the results from one market timing model in effect since 1970 versus a buy and hold New York Stock Exchange Index strategy (See Chart 12-1). An initial investment of $100,000 for the buy and hold strategy grew to $3.9 million yielding a compounded annual return of 12.0 percent. In comparison, the $100,000 invested under the Timing Model rose to $7.5 million after all expenses and management fees for a compounded annual return of 14.2 percent. More importantly, the timing model outperformed the buy and hold strategy on a risk-adjusted basis. Of course, past model results are no guarantee of future returns.

# Chart 12-1

## PERFORMANCE SUMMARY
### 1/1/1970 to 6/30/2002

| | Comp. Annual Return | Net Annual Return | $100,000 Inv. Now Worth | Volatility 'Beta' | Risk Adj. Superiority Index 'Alpha' |
|---|---|---|---|---|---|
| MANAGED (NYSE) | 15.60% | 14.20% | 7,505,672 | 0.435 | 5.251 |
| | | | | | |
| Buy and Hold (NYSE) | | 12.00% | 3,925,088 | 1 | 0 |

*Courtesy of SIMCO*
*NYSE=New York Stock Exchange Total Return Index*
*See Appendix C for Disclosure Statement*

There should be several evident conclusions from the presentation in this chart.

1. While risk will always remain a part of investing in the stock market and losses cannot be eliminated, active risk management tactics possess the potential to reduce risks down to levels acceptable by many investors.
2. An important by-product of these risk reduction strategies permits potentially higher returns, especially on a risk-adjusted basis.

**"Accumulation of wealth may be a matter of time, but I strongly believe that lasting wealth is a matter of timing."**

*—John K. Sosnowy*

Active risk management consists of measuring the direction of a market or market index and moving funds in or out of the market based on those measurements. Classic market timing usually involves 100 percent moves between equities and cash. The market timing strategy of using other asset classes in addition to equities and cash to take advantage of market changes is called tactical asset allocation.

The goal of all timing strategies is to reduce risk and deliver higher returns on a risk-adjusted basis. You want to manage risk instead of avoiding it by hiding your assets in savings accounts, money market accounts, certificates of deposit, and T-Bills as Connie Conservative did. As we saw in Myth #4, Connie's strategy failed to keep up with the ravages of inflation and taxes.

Through the use of time-tested econometric models, active risk managers try to be in position to purchase stocks when the emotional sellers are selling and dispose of stocks when the emotional buyers are buying. Through computer simulations, we have tested active management market timing models as far back as 1927 as we showed in Chart 5-2 (others have tested them back as much as 100 years, as we showed in Myth #8), and the results have been extremely encouraging.

In fact, at least two published studies, the first by Jerry Wagner, Steve Shellans, and Rich Paul in the *Journal of Portfolio Management* (1992), and the second by Professors Don Chance of Virginia Tech and Michael Hemler of Notre Dame (2001) have demonstrated the value of active risk management. In the conclusions section of their study, Chance and Hemler state, "We provide new evidence regarding the ability of professional market timers . . . . Contrary to most prior research, we find significant ability across all tests and portfolios . . . . We believe three factors explain why this study, unlike most of its predecessors, finds evidence of timing ability. First, the timers studied here are professionals who actually execute their recommendations for clients . . . . Second, because the recommendations studied here are explicitly known, they are free of estimation error . . . . Third, the recommendations studied here are observed daily, not monthly or quarterly."

**"Look for people with a solid system and (the) discipline to stick with their indicators."**

*—Robert Farrell*
*Merrill, Lynch, Pierce, Fenner, & Smith*

Active risk management is a disciplined approach for reducing the risk of stock market investing. While the average investor may not be able to practice active risk management themselves because they let emotions get in the way of rational action, active risk management can work in the hands of a disciplined professional. Don't let the confusion over the definition of active risk management or the naysayers, who have not been able to figure out how to use it properly, discourage you from evaluating its contributions to achieving solid risk-adjusted returns. You have a choice. You can sit back with a buy and hold strategy and watch the bear market chew up your portfolio or employ an active risk management professional to help you reduce risk and conserve your portfolio assets for investment when the market turns around.

## Key Points to Remember:

- The idea that everyone is going to buy and hold through a disastrous bear market is outrageous.
- Active risk management market timing is a legitimate investment strategy with proven results over more than thirty years.
- Through computer simulations, timing models have been tested back as far as 100 years, and the results have been extremely encouraging.

# MYTH #13

## The stock market can be counted on to make me 10-12 percent per year.

"We find buy and hold to be highly overrated as an investment approach, perhaps due to false confidence based on hindsight analysis and underestimation of the risks associated with long and severe drawdown periods."

*—Robert W. Colby and Thomas A. Meyers*
*The Encyclopedia of Technical Market Indicators*

While the total return averages for the broad market have averaged 10-12 percent per year for the past 75 years, there have been extended periods of under-performance as well as over-performance.

Many analysts are debating whether comparisons should be made between the current bear market, 2000-02, and 1973-74, or whether this market is closer to the rare exceptions of 1929-31 in the U.S. and 1989-92 in Japan. In my opinion, the debate may really be a moot point, because the aftermath of each of these three market debacles is very similar. In the ten years after 1929-31, the Dow made only 3.22 percent per year. In the eight years after 1974, the Dow made only 1.70 percent per year (and the S&P 500 only 4.70 percent per year). From 1989-

92, the Japanese market dropped 60 percent. In the ten years after 1992, the Japanese market has lost another 37 percent. This means that if the NASDAQ (whose bubble of the 1990's is often compared to the Japanese Nikkei of the 1980's) were to follow the same pattern, the NASDAQ composite index would still be at or below 1328 in the year 2012.

The point here is not to scare you, but to make sure you understand that it is not a "gimmie" that the NASDAQ has to bounce back to 5000, or 2500, or even 2000 anytime soon. While historically, both in time and in percentages, we should be close to a market bottom, we may be many years from the next "great" bull market.

Therefore, if you are fully invested in the stock market, it is unrealistic to expect 10-12 percent returns year after year. While that may be the average over the long haul, it cannot be counted on to make you those returns on an annual basis. In any one year, returns on the S&P 500 have been as high as +50 percent and as low as -45 percent. And, remember, when you do have the down years, it takes a long time to make up that loss, not to mention, an even longer time to begin to turn a profit.

Buy and hold investing has theoretically provided enough return to offset taxes and inflation, but very few investors have the emotional strength to ride out all the ups and downs of the stock market. This strategy can literally wipe you out if a bear market occurs after you retire and are making regular withdrawals.

Remember Peter Hope from Myth #11. He employed a buy and hold investment strategy, suffered through a devastating bear market, and ended up destitute. The investment misadventures of Peter Hope clearly point out the dangers of ignoring active risk management as a key component of your investment plans.

In the November/December 2002 issue of AARP's *Modern Maturity* magazine, CNN *Moneyline* anchor Lou Dobbs had the following exchange with AARP's Susan Adams:

*Q. What advice would you give to investors at a time like this?*

*A. Sell your investment if it loses 10 percent. I can't tell you the number of investment advisors I hear saying, "Make your selection for the long term." To me, that's an absolutely foolish approach.*

It sounds to me like Lou Dobbs advocates active risk management versus buy and hold, also.

## Key Points to Remember:

- While the stock market may average returns of 10-12 percent over the long haul, you cannot expect to consistently have those kinds of returns each and every year.
- When you have big down years, it can take an extremely long time just to get back to breakeven.
- The buy and hold strategy can literally wipe you out if a bear market occurs after you retire and are making regular withdrawals.

# MYTH #14

## I'll never make any money in a down market.

**"There will always be bull markets followed by bear markets followed by bull markets followed by bear markets but the long-term trend is up."**

*—Sir John Templeton*

Whether the trend of the stock market is up or down, there are opportunities for profit if you are willing to take the risk of investing on both the long and short side of the market.

For the more aggressive investor, there may be the desire not only to exit the stock market at an opportune time, but also to figure out a way to have the opportunity to make more than a money market return in down markets, too! Now there is a practical strategy for taking advantage of downside market moves. It is through the use of what I call an 'inverse' fund, that is, a mutual fund whose investment results are specifically designed to inversely correlate with a major market average, such as the S&P 500. This means that on a day when the S&P 500 index is down in value "x" percent, an S&P 500 inverse fund should be up in value "x" percent and vice versa.

To test the feasibility of such a strategy, I performed computer simulations back to 1927. To accomplish this test, I enhanced my basic risk management model with an algorithm for timing the use of the inverse fund. I was very encouraged by the results. Over sixty-nine years, using the S&P 500 as the stock fund and the inverse of the S&P 500 as the inverse fund, you could have earned three times as much money as you would without the use of the inverse fund and almost forty times as much as an investor buying and holding the S&P 500 basket of stocks over the same time frame. More importantly, some of the very best returns were in the exceptionally poor market periods.

In his book, *Conquer the Crash*, Robert R. Prechter, Jr. also discusses the benefit of investing in inverse funds. Just as I said earlier, Prechter points out that inverse funds, also called short funds or bear funds, are an investment vehicle designed to capitalize on falling stock indexes. In the U.S., you will find inverse S&P 500 index funds at Rydex (www.rydexfunds.com) and ProFunds (www.profunds.com). Rydex has Ursa, which is the largest inverse index fund available, and ProFunds has the Bear ProFund. Rydex also has Arktos, which moves inversely to the NASDAQ 100 Index, and Venture, which trades twice daily and is designed to replicate two times the inverse of the NASDAQ 100. ProFunds has its Short OTC and Ultra Short OTC Funds.

The companies that offer inverse funds also offer money market funds, bond funds, and long index and enhanced index funds, too; so with a brief phone call, you can easily move your money to take advantage of swings in either direction or park it for safety. By the way, Rydex's money market fund owns only instruments issued, guaranteed, or backed by the U.S. government or its agencies or instrumentalities, making it safer than the average money market fund, and ProFunds has a money market fund rated AAAm by Standard and Poors.

## Portfolio Managers Who Are Not Afraid To Be Bearish

I don't claim to know every professional money manager who has a long and short strategy, but both SIMCO (1-800-526-2152, www.lastingwealth.com) and Flexible Plan Investments, Ltd. (1-800-347-3539, www.flexibleplan.com) offer a daily trading strategy that utilizes a model that first started trading in February 2001, which utilizes the Rydex Dynamic Funds, Velocity (long) and Venture (inverse).

Since inception (through 10/15/2002), this strategy has made a return after fees in excess of 40 percent in actual accounts versus a loss of over 64 percent for its benchmark, the NASDAQ 100 Index, during the same period. Note that the range of returns included double-digit drawdowns as well. [See Appendix D for Disclosure Statement.]

They also have a similar trading strategy designed for use with variable annuity products. The model used for this strategy started actual trading within American Skandia (www.americanskandia.com) annuities in July 2001 and uses ProFunds sub-accounts, and since then they have also used this model at Nationwide Marketflex (www.bestofamerica.com) and Security Benefit Advisor Designs (www.securitybenefit.com) using Rydex sub-accounts. Since inception (through 10/15/2002), it had a performance after fees of -2 percent versus -46 percent for its benchmark, the NASDAQ 100 Index. [See Appendix D for Disclosure Statement.]

While neither of these models have been used in actual trading for a long period of time, I believe that they have passed their initial test in a very difficult down market environment, thus supporting my earlier historical research. Of course, past performance is no guarantee of future results. Please ask for and examine a prospectus for the aforementioned funds and/or annuities before you invest.

Models like these are best suited for the investor with high income and/or net worth, no current income needs, one who understands and accepts the volatility and risks inherent in 100 percent exposure to NASDAQ-oriented, enhanced index stock funds on a daily model buy and/or inverse signal, and who understands that these are very actively traded strategies best suited for tax qualified and/or tax-deferred accounts.

## Key Points to Remember:

- It is possible to make money in a down market if you are a more aggressive investor.
- A practical strategy for taking advantage of downside market moves is through the use of an inverse fund, a mutual fund whose investment results are specifically designed to inversely correlate with a major market average, such as the S&P 500 or the NASDAQ 100.
- NASDAQ-oriented funds are more practical for use in a daily trading model utilizing an inverse fund.

# MYTH #15

## With the information available to me today, I don't need professional advice. I can do it myself.

"Many a man or woman who would not expect to be successful as a circus clown, opera singer, or grocer, without some kind of preparation or talent, nevertheless expects to be successful right off in the stock market—probably the most intricate and difficult game on earth. The reason for this faith in success without any special qualification is doubtless the most universal belief in luck."

—*Fred Kelley*
*Why You Win and Lose*

It is unrealistic to expect an individual working to keep the income flowing and trying to build net worth also to be able to continually analyze the health of the economy and the stock market, to track 10,000 mutual funds, to stay on top of multiple asset classes and their relative valuations, and to follow rapidly expanding global opportunities (the U.S. only accounts for about 20 percent of the world's economy) in order to effectively manage his or her own money over the long term.

"The market level does not, as so many imagine, represent the consensus judgment of experts who have carefully weighed the long-term evidence. The market is high (or low) because of the combined effect of indifferent thinking by millions of people, very few of whom feel the need to perform careful research . . . . Their all-too-human behavior is heavily influenced by news media that are interested in attracting viewers or readers, with limited incentive to discipline their readers with the type of quantitative analysis that might give them a correct impression of the aggregate stock market level."

—*Robert J. Shiller*
*Irrational Exuberance*

With more money to invest and a greater dependence on the results of those investments for their retirement nest eggs, people are seeking financial advice in record numbers and rightly so. Some estimates place direct purchases by investors, without the advice of a broker or financial advisor, as accounting for as little as 15 percent of the total in the $2.8 trillion mutual fund industry.

Every person has a circle of competence . . . things that they do well. If you make your living as a product development manager in a computer software company, you are probably going to be hard pressed to make a living being a concert pianist. If you need brain surgery, you don't attempt it yourself moonlighting as a brain surgeon. Instead, you find the best brain surgeon available. You have probably heard the old adage, a person serving as his or her own lawyer has a fool for a client. I have found that the most successful people operate within their own

circle of competence and hire outside professionals
to work for them in areas outside of that arena. Likewise, you need a full-time, experienced, professional,
disciplined investment advisor to take the emotions
out of your investment decisions.

Building a good relationship with a financial advisor, however, isn't always easy. To accomplish this,
it is helpful to understand the feelings you might
experience when you meet with an advisor. First of
all, trust needs to form a key aspect in the relationship. It is normal to initially worry that the person
across the table is just giving you a line in hopes of
trying to sell you something and take your money.

It is also very difficult for many people to openly
discuss their financial situations. Talking about
money still remains taboo for many in our society,
thus exposing your financial situation to a stranger
may feel uncomfortable. To add to this discomfort,
your advisor is required by law and regulation to
ask a number of questions, which you may consider
to be very nosy, to determine the suitability of different investment options for you.

You may also fear looking foolish in front of the
advisor. As a respected professional in your field, it
can be difficult to admit that you have not managed
your money as well as you have managed other as-
pects of your life, such as your career. The reality is
that very few people have the time or inclination to
be experts at many different subjects. Finally, even
relatively well-off individuals often do not believe that
they have enough money to interest a professional
financial advisor.

You need to overcome those fears and uncertain-
ties to make the relationship with your advisor work.
First and foremost, ask your advisor questions. The
only dumb question is the one that does not get

asked. You need to establish a comfort level with the advisor by gaining an understanding of his or her background and financial expertise. Don't be afraid to ask uncomfortable questions such as how he or she has invested money for their own account or what investments they have found most profitable or least successful. Inquire why he or she became an investment advisor and what professional background and experience led them to this position.

Make sure you understand the advisor's investment approach and what the worst case scenario might be using that approach. Is that a risk you could accept? Does your investment time frame fit the advisor's investment methods? How is the advisor compensated for managing your money? Does the advisor have access to your funds and under what circumstances? Could your money end up in the advisor's office decorations or seaside condo? If you are not comfortable with the responses to your questions, look elsewhere for an advisor. Remember, your gut feelings or instincts with people often prove right. Find someone with whom you can work comfortably.

Time represents one of the most important elements of a successful investment strategy. You must be willing to give the strategy and the investment advisor adequate time to make it work for you.

**"You can't expect to see calves running in the field the day after you put the bull in the pasture."**

*—Texas rancher*

Constantly changing advisors in search of the perfect fit will end up hurting performance more than it helps. There are many different investment advisors and investment approaches from which to choose. Take the time up front to find one who fits your financial needs and goals and do not be afraid to tell a prospective advisor that you do not think it would be a good fit. If the person gets insulted by your comment, take that as a good indication that he or she is definitely not right for you.

If this is your first venture with a financial advisor, you do not have to trust all of your funds to your new investment advisor. While most advisors charge a sliding scale of fees that benefits the client who has more money under management, it may make sense for you to start with a smaller initial investment and later add to that amount as your confidence in the advisor and his or her strategies increases.

You get what you pay for, so do not base your investment advisor decision on fees alone. Look at the total picture. While it is unwise to pay too much, it can be a disaster to pay too little and lose a major part of your investment or even everything.

**"It isn't as important to buy as cheap as possible as it is to buy at the right time."**

*—Jesse Livermore*

## Turn Off The TV

Due to modern technology, the average person has access to a plethora of information regarding stocks, trends, mergers, and every other kind of news or opinions you can imagine. This information can take an investor on a very frustrating roller coaster ride if he or she is not careful. The following excerpt from *The Fortune Tellers* by Howard Kurtz is a good example of what can happen:

> *Let's say you want to invest in Schlock.com. You study the company's business plan, gauge its future, look at where the stock price is and where it was last month and last year. Then you take the plunge and buy 100 shares at $50 a share. Two weeks later, Maria Bartiromo comes on the air and reports that some Morgan Stanley analyst you've never heard of is downgrading the stock; it drops five points. A week later, Gene Marcial discloses in Business Week that Schlock.com is a potential takeover target for Supersoft Industries; the stock jumps 10 points, but slumps by 15 when no merger takes place. Then there is talk in an Internet chat room that Barron's may be coming out with a negative piece on Schlock.com; it drops another 3 points, even though the article turns out to be mildly favorable. Two months later, Schlock reports $100 million in earnings, twice as much as a year ago, but Wall Street analysts moan because the per-share earning is two cents less than they, in their wisdom, had expected. The stock drops 12 points, and Jim Cramer writes a Street.com piece about how he hates the CEO and has sold all his holdings. Whenever the company is discussed on CNBC, they flash a yellow chart with the lines heading south. You finally dump it for a $2,500 loss. The next week, the Journal's Heard on the Street column says the company is bringing out a new generation of schlock and the stock jumps 14 points while you gnash your teeth.*

That's the maddening reality of a market where a gust of rhetorical wind can buffet your stock like a sailboat in a hurricane. Over time, of course, good companies perform well and justify their stockholders' investment. But in a wired world where everyone is looking for a short-term edge, it's all too easy to get upended by a small group of experts whose self-interest is not always apparent.

*Beyond the brokers and the analysts, online colum-
nists and advocates have all sorts of motivations and
questionable sources, and hardly anyone to hold them
accountable. Journalists fan the rumor flames in search
of a hot story, and rarely bother to follow up on the analysts' ratings that they repeat like the day's mantra, even
when the calls turn out to be flat wrong. The media act as
a great seducer ("The Best Mutual Funds!", "Secrets of
the Stock Stars!"), luring people to tune in or log on or
open their checkbooks on the promise of major paydays
to come. And yet these are the shaky reeds on which millions of investment decisions rest.*

This scenario precisely demonstrates the value
of professional risk management services. I encourage you to turn off the TV, put down the newspaper,
and entrust your money and investment decisions
to a professional. Chances are that you will rest much
easier if you do . . . and make more return over the
long haul!

## Avoid The Stock Tip Scam

There is a mail, e-mail, and/or fax scam that
was exposed by Thom Hartle, former editor of *Stocks
& Commodities* magazine. Here goes: Over the course
of 10 weeks, say you received five anonymous stock
tips in the mail. The instructions would arrive on
Wednesday, advising you to place a trade that Friday, hold for the week, and exit the following Friday.
Then the next Wednesday, a new tip would arrive.
All five trades were profitable—a remarkable feat.
Then, a pitch arrived for a $1,000 newsletter prom-
ising more trades with the same format of winning
instructions. The potential winnings in the five
trades came to more than $13,000, and each trade
was given without the benefit of hindsight! This stock

tip service looks too good to be true. And it *is* too good to be true, but how does someone pull this off?

He—or she—does it like this. The tipster is an unscrupulous character out to profit from the public's keen interest in trading stocks. It's a simple process. The first step: the tipster gets hold of a list of 20,000 names and addresses. He or she then picks a volatile stock and sends out the anonymous tips. The trick here is that 10,000 people get a buy tip, while 10,000 people get advice to sell the stock short. After the one-week holding period, half of the postcard recipients have a profitable trade while the other half have a loser.

The same process will be repeated the following week, but the losers are dropped from that mailing. That mailing will be to just the 10,000 people who received a correct forecast from the original list of 20,000 names. Again, the list is split in two: 5,000 people will be told to buy on Friday and hold till the following Friday, while 5,000 will be told to go short that Friday and exit the next.

The Fridays come and go, and, at this point, we have 5,000 people who now have had two winning tips. The tipster repeats the process again, ending up with the number of winners down to 2,500. Then one more go-round and we have 1,250, and finally, one last cut for 625 winners. After that, there are now 625 people who have received what appear to be five perfect forecasts of winning trades in the stock market. The greed of those 625 is fueled, so the next step is to hit them with the sales pitch for the $1,000 newsletter. How many of those 625 people will be willing, if not downright eager, to part with $1,000 to continue this winning streak? A good many. Do you think that anyone will see any profit after they send in the $1,000? Not likely.

In this story, it appears that the track record is real-time forecasting, but it is after-the-fact manipulation of the data, and that's why it looks so good. With today's market volatility, it's easy for people to let their desire for profit cloud their judgment.

It goes without saying that succumbing to greed is not new!

The point: Know who you are doing business with. Make sure they have a real-time verifiable track record.

## You Need An Advisor Now More Than Ever

In this Internet, information-at-your-fingertips age, some say that financial advisors and money managers are obsolete go-betweens. However, Allan Sloan's article, "Long Live the Middleman," in the June 14, 1999 issue of *Newsweek* says not to bury them yet.

The more information that's available online, the more valuable competent advisors and middlemen become. There's a big difference between information and knowledge. Someone has to filter out the information from the noise and do something useful with it. The more information there is, the more choices there are, and the harder it is to make a decision. Online trading is fine if you know what you want to buy or sell, and you are not worried about getting clobbered during volatile markets. But if you do not know what to do, a good, smart, honest financial advisor or money manager is more important than ever.

Steve Shellans of the *MoniResearch Newsletter* (www.moniresearch.com) addressed the same issue in the September 1997 issue of *Stocks & Commodities*. "I know from experience it takes a lot more effort and resources and money than most people think to develop a successful model. So if somebody wants to develop a model as a hobby, for personal interest and for the technical challenge involved, fine. But if they're doing it for financial reasons, either to avoid paying a professional manager a few dollars or because he thinks he can do better than the professional money managers, it is my opinion that he is ill-advised." He continues, "When an investor retains a money manager and gives him or her the money to manage, he or she can go about their business, go on vacations, whatever." And finally, "The last consideration is one of ego. When you develop your own model and you have a losing trade, and believe me, a lot of trades will be losing trades, no matter how good you are, you'll have ego problems. Whereas if you have a professional money manager, you're one step removed. It's less immediate and doesn't affect your ego." The *MoniResearch Newsletter* has been tracking the performance of active managers for twenty-two (22) years.

## Amid Recent Corporate Scandals, Professional Money Management Is Essential

In the August 2002 issue of *Financial Planning* magazine, Len Reinhart takes a look at today's cold, hard corporate world. Sometimes, you just have to shake your head and wonder, "What were they thinking?" A successful entrepreneur, at the helm of a $400 million company, sacrifices his personal image and jeopardizes the company's future to save a few hundred thousand dollars in stock market losses. Another multimillionaire executive risks jail time to avoid a million in legitimate taxes.

The inescapable lesson of these unnerving events

is that affluent, successful people should insulate themselves by using a professional money manager, or multiple money managers, to execute their financial plan and their investing activities.

If managers cannot rely on the numbers that drive stock selection, they can protect their clients from catastrophic loss by making sure that no one company represents a significant portion of an individual's total wealth. In addition, the money manager provides insulation between the investor and the buy-and-sell decisions in the portfolio. If someone else is making the decisions, it is unlikely that anyone will accuse the individual of trading improprieties.

Think about it. Why was Martha Stewart trading individual stocks through a broker? She has (or had) far too much money to be managing it piecemeal, and essentially by herself. For people at this level of affluence to depend on their personal knowledge and on-the-fly decision-making is enormously risky. Professional management is not a luxury for these individuals—it's an essential.

## Key Points to Remember:

- Today, it is more important than ever to seek professional advice. There is a big difference between information and knowledge.
- You need a full-time, experienced, professional, and disciplined investment advisor to take the emotions out of your investment decisions for you.
- Time represents one of the most important elements of a successful investment strategy. You must be willing to give the strategy and

the investment advisor adequate time to make it work for you.

- Turn off the TV, put down the newspaper, and entrust your money and investment decisions to a professional.
- Know who you are doing business with. Make sure your investment advisor has a real-time verifiable track record.
- Professional management is not a luxury for affluent individuals—it's an essential.

# MYTH #16

## After no more than one year, I should be able to evaluate whether my investment approach is working or not.

"There are many reasons not to chase after last year's hot investment, be it a mutual fund, variable annuity, or whatever. But the most important reason is that there is no earthly way of discerning if one year's performance is meaningful at all. Instead, look at long-term performance."

—*Gary Belsky and Thomas Gilovich*
*Why Smart People Make Big Money Mistakes*

### Patience, Patience, Patience

Like so many things in life, there is no right way or wrong way to invest all of the time. Investing styles represent a matter of personality and personal risk tolerance and goals. What works for one person may not be appropriate for another. But no matter what investment approach you decide to use, or whether you plan to develop and follow your own set of indicators or hire a professional money manager, one thing remains true. You will need to exercise a great deal of patience. I advise giving your investment approach at least one complete market cycle to work.

That usually covers five years at the minimum, ten years would be even better.

**"After spending many years in Wall Street and making and losing millions of dollars I want to tell you this: It was never my thinking that made the big money for me. It was always my sitting. Got that? My sitting tight! It is not a trick to be all right on the market. You always find lots of early bulls in bull markets and early bears in bear markets . . . . Men who can both be right and sit tight are uncommon. I found it one of the hardest things to learn. That is why so many men in Wall Street, who are not at all in the sucker class . . . nevertheless lose money. The market does not beat them. They beat themselves because though they have brains, they cannot sit tight."**

*—Jesse Livermore, famous stock speculator*
*Reminiscences of a Stock Operator*

Time is an essential factor in the success of any investment strategy because there is no such thing as an infallible investment. With any investment strategy, including active risk management, you are going to have your share of winners and losers. The critical thing is to develop an investment approach based on good, sound reasoning and to allow it enough time to work so that the winners outnumber the losers.

Changing horses in midstream often results in drowning. Likewise, changing course, moving on to a new investment approach, or switching investment managers every time you suffer a loss will extract a heavy toll on your portfolio performance in terms of fees and transaction costs, as well as lost benefits from the learning curve. Instead of abandoning your investment approach too early, use the time to continually refine and fine tune it. Every investment management strategy has its strengths and weaknesses. Too often, to their detriment, investors tend to join a manager right after a period of strength and quit following a period of weakness, just as they often do in buying and selling mutual funds.

In order for an active risk management strategy to have a chance to outperform the market, you have to experience periods of down markets. It is during these times, when the investor is able to avoid the biggest portion of a major decline and move back into the market with much of his or her capital intact, that active risk management has the potential to deliver its greatest reward.

Before you adopt an investment approach or consider changing it, ask yourself the following series of questions:

1. Does the investment approach make sense to you? Do you understand how it should work and believe in the underlying principles (not the intricacies or all the details) of the approach?

2. Are the reasons you first decided to follow the investment approach still valid? While you want to give the approach enough time to work, do not be blindsided by dramatically changing economic and market conditions which make the premises, upon which your original strategy is based, useless.

3. Do you trust the investment manager's (or your own) ability to implement the program? Has the manager been in business long enough for his approach to be time-tested

over a variety of different economic sce-
narios?
4. What is the worst possible scenario or outcome from the investment approach? Can you
live with that outcome?

In the investing world, there's always the temp-
tation to jump to the latest hot trend, the widely
hailed hot pick. The problem with this approach is
that the hot fund or idea has probably already made
its major move. Following the crowd can be much
like being one of the last people in a pyramid scheme.
Remember the word hot means there's a good likelihood that you can get burned.

Being successful frequently means looking for
opportunities away from the maddening crowd and
sticking with those investments until the reason you
first found them attractive materializes or until it is
clear the investment plan is never going to come to
fruition. Otherwise, if everything is performing as it
was designed, then stay the course.

As I have said before, time represents one of the
most important elements of a successful investment
strategy. You must be willing to give the strategy
and the investment advisor adequate time to make
it work for you.

**"Ignore short term performance and focus in-
stead on performance over many years."**

*—Mark Hulbert*
**Hulbert Financial Digest**

"There is virtually no correlation between past
and future performance over a one-year period," according to respected financial writer and analyst,

Mark Hulbert. In fact, Hulbert's study of correlations between past and future performance shows that the correlation only gets above 50 percent after 8 years.

## Chart 16-1

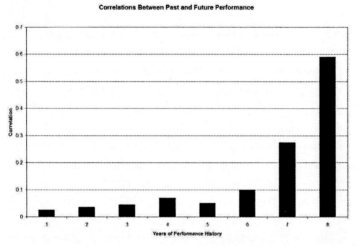

Correlations Between Past and Future Performance

*Presented by Mark Hulbert, Seattle Money Show, October 23, 1998*

Mark Hulbert makes three conclusions regarding his study of correlations between past and future performance:

1. In no event should you look at performance less than five years.
2. Eight years or more of data looks most promising.
3. Go for as much historical data as possible!

## Key Points to Remember:

- You should give your investment approach at least one complete market cycle to work. That usually covers five years at the minimum, ten years would be even better.
- Time is an essential factor in the success of any investment strategy because there is no such thing as an infallible investment.
- It has been proven that last year's top performers are seldom the following year's winners.

# MYTH #17

## Variable annuities are for fools.

"Mutual funds and annuities are complementary, not mutually exclusive investments. The only significant difference between the two is that in variable annuity contracts, mutual funds are called sub-accounts."

*—Bruce F. Wells*
*All about Variable Annuities*

Variable annuities are usually funded with after-tax contributions, all earnings are tax-deferred, they have virtually no contribution limits, and no requirement to begin withdrawals at a certain age. It should be noted, however, that many variable annuities have ages after which certain benefits are forfeited, such as enhanced death benefits.

### Benefits of Variable Annuities

Since keeping the tax man at bay can pay tremendous benefits in the form of higher portfolio values, it is appropriate here to review the benefits of one form of tax-deferral that anyone can use . . . variable annuities, an investment you should not overlook, especially if you are approaching your retirement years.

**"It is prudent to keep funds liquid but liquidity often has its price: current taxes."**

*—James Sheperdson III, President*
*Endeavor Series Trust*

After Congress passed the Taxpayer Relief Act of 1997, which changed the capital gains tax rates that apply to individual investments, some investors thought that variable annuities had lost their biggest advantage. The National Association for Variable Annuities (NAVA) retained Price Waterhouse to analyze the impact of this tax legislation on variable annuities.

"The study confirms the fundamental superiority of the annuity product as a retirement planning vehicle," said NAVA President and CEO Mark J. Mackey. "Tax deferral helps investments grow faster and the pay-out options help them last longer."

The study found that people seeking long-term investments benefit from choosing variable annuities over mutual funds. Dr. Peter Merrill, director of the study and national director of tax policy economics for Price Waterhouse, said, "After-tax pay-outs from variable annuities are substantially larger than mutual fund investments even for holding periods as short as 10 years."

If you got a late start on saving for retirement or have decided that the amount of money you have accumulated to date is not going to last you through your retirement years, one means of increasing the potential return on your investments and the amount of financial assets you will have available at retirement is the variable annuity.

Baby boomers, looking ahead to retirement, are taking this message to heart. Variable annuity sales have skyrocketed over the past several years, bolstered by the coming of age of the baby boom generation. According to the VARDS (Variable Annuity Research and Data Service) Report, variable annuity sales reached $113 billion in 2001. In fact, sales have risen from $10 billion in 1989 to the $113 billion in 2001.

A number of factors are behind this explosive growth. To be sure, the sustained bull market during the 1990's drew many new investors. Likewise, the growth of mutual funds has expanded investment choices within variable annuities while 401(k) plans have taught investors the value of tax-deferred investing. Enhanced variable annuity products have also played a role in attracting new customers.

Finally, the coming of age of the baby boom generation represents a prime market for variable annuities. Baby boomers are using variable annuities as a way to grow their retirement assets efficiently while taking advantage of their tax-deferral benefits.

A variable annuity is an insurance contract with a different twist. This tax-deferred retirement vehicle is issued by an insurance carrier that offers diversified investment options (called sub-accounts) and includes life insurance protection. Unlike its distant cousin, the fixed annuity, the variable annuity does not guarantee a minimum interest rate over the contract lifetime. However, it does permit investment in equities through a variety of investment options, thereby giving the investor an opportunity to participate in the stock market which has traditionally outperformed other forms of investments over the long-term. The variable annuity value is determined by the changing value of the underlying portfolio of debt and equity sub-accounts.

The underlying portfolio of sub-accounts typically looks and performs just like a family of mutual funds. Today, many mutual fund companies offer variable annuities in conjunction with an insurance company, where the underlying investments mirror well-known funds and are, in fact, managed by the same portfolio managers. Obviously, there are additional costs associated with the variable annuity to cover the mortality risk of the insurance company.

Under the fixed annuity contract, the insurance company assumes the investment risk while variable annuity investors shoulder the market risk in anticipation of enhancing their investment return and boosting their retirement distribution amount. The purchase of a variable annuity can be tailored to the individual's financial situation offering either a lump sum payment or a series of installment payments.

The longer your money is invested in a variable annuity, the greater the benefit of tax-deferral. At the end of twenty years, a $100,000 investment returning 10 percent annually and taxed at 31 percent would have grown to $379,799. Tax-deferred, that same $100,000 would have grown to $672,750. After paying 31 percent in taxes, you would still have $495,197 left, an increase in earnings of 41 percent. If you look at the same investment after thirty years, the taxable investment would have grown to $740,169 versus a value of $1,235,009 for the tax-deferred annuity after payment of 31 percent in taxes. That's a 77 percent greater gain.

Another tax saving attribute of variable annuities is the ability of investors to switch investments between sub-accounts (investment options within the annuity) without triggering a taxable event as would be the case in a regular mutual fund. Within multi-manager annuities you can even change fund families without any current tax consequences. The tax-free exchange of investment assets also permits the contract holder to utilize active risk management techniques or market timing without setting off a taxable event. Talk about having your cake and eating it, too! IRS regulations provide for even greater flexibility. Under IRS Code Section 1035, variable annuity holders may even switch insurance carriers while maintaining the tax-deferral.

Compared with other retirement vehicles such as IRA's, SEP's, and 401(k)'s, variable annuity investors are not limited to minimal amounts of annual contributions nor do contributions have to be made from earned income. One million dollars or more annually can be contributed to most variable annuities. However, since contributions to IRA's, SEP's, and 401(k)'s are generally tax deductible, they should be funded first.

Expanded death benefit features represent another attraction of variable annuities. Greater annual step-ups of the minimum death benefit provides a fail-safe value no matter how aggressive an investment stance the annuity holder takes.

In general, minimum death benefits guarantee the contract holder with a minimum payout in case of death, no matter how poorly the investment portfolio may be performing at the time of death. Thus, it protects against downward market fluctuations by locking in a minimum payout. The minimum death benefit is typically calculated as the greater of the contract value at the time of death, the highest account value on any contract anniversary (plus subsequent investments), or the amount contributed plus an effective annual yield. A stepped-up death benefit is reset to equal the account value, typically every seven years, while the rolled-up death benefit is increased by a certain percentage, typically 4 or 5 percent, every year regardless of fund performance. Variable annuity death benefits also avoid probate by passing directly to the named beneficiary.

Variable annuities provide a degree of security not afforded to owners of fixed annuities. Unlike fixed annuities which are general insurance company assets, variable annuity investments are separate assets held by a trustee and cannot be attached by creditors in the event the insurance company fails. And in some states, variable annuities are also judgment proof and cannot be attached by the creditors of the owner of the annuity. However, there are contract guarantees that may not survive bankruptcies.

Variable annuities are geared toward investors with a long-term focus on retirement planning. Surrender charges for early withdrawal of funds discourage redemptions and encourage letting the money perform its job of building retirement funds. Like retirement accounts, except under certain circumstances, you cannot withdraw variable annuity funds prior to age 59 1/2 without incurring a 10 percent tax penalty. However, you can delay beginning withdrawals from the annuity until age 90 or even longer in some cases, compared to age 70 1/2 with tax-deferred retirement accounts. Depending on your personal financial situation, this could be a very important feature.

Surrender charges can amount to as much as 9 percent in the early years with a downward sliding scale to zero after seven years or so, depending on the contract; however, some variable annuities to-

day have a no surrender charge option. A stiff surrender charge can be a significant drawback should
circumstances force the withdrawal of money during the early years of the contract, but most variable annuities allow a 10 percent free withdrawal
each year. Obviously, incurring surrender charges
can entirely wipe out or substantially reduce investment returns. Therefore, it's important you invest
with a long-term perspective.

The annuity aspect comes into play when you
decide to start withdrawing your retirement funds.
A variety of payout options gives investors the ability to plan their retirement income the way they want
to receive it. At that time, you can either make ir-
regular or systematic withdrawals while leaving your
investment in the variable annuity account, or you
can annuitize the account.

Among annuity payout options are a single lump
sum payment, lifetime annuity (you receive income
for the remainder of your life), joint lifetime annuity
(you and your spouse receive income as long as either of you is alive), and a lifetime annuity with a
minimum number of payments guaranteed. Should
you die before you receive the prescribed minimum
number of payments, your beneficiary will receive
the balance. With a variable annuity, if your heir is
also your spouse, he or she can opt to continue the
annuity and further postpone withdrawals and taxes.

Another advantage of an annuity is the ability of
the beneficiary to stretch out payments (and thus
payment of taxes on gains) far into the future after
the death of the contract owner. If you, as owner, die
before the annuity start date and your spouse is not
your beneficiary, the default rule requires that the
entire balance of the contract be distributed to the
designated beneficiary within five years. However, if

the beneficiary wishes to extend the payment of benefits as long as possible, he or she can elect the alternative life expectancy method, which requires distributions to begin within one year of death but allows payments to be stretched out over the entire life expectancy of the beneficiary.

It's easy to get into a variable annuity. Typically, only a $1,000 minimum initial investment is required. Subsequent investments can be as low as $50. However, the average initial investment is approximately $20,000.

Of course there are some trade-offs to consider. Variable annuities carry an additional fee, the mortality and expense (M&E) charge, not present in a mutual fund. Shop around for the best deal in terms of overall product and fees. Be sure to ask for and carefully examine the prospectus for all costs, fees, and terms. These fees typically total 2.2 percent annually on a $25,000 investment, compared to an average 1.4 percent for a mutual fund. For this reason, annuities work best with growth stock funds that offer higher potential long-term returns. In these funds, the additional fees are often offset by superior performance. I believe this occurs because funds under the variable annuity umbrella are often smaller and thus more nimble than their retail counterparts. In addition, variable annuity investors typically take a longer term investment focus and cause less turnover problems for the portfolio manager.

John P. Huggard, J.D., CFP, and professor in the Department of Business Management at North Carolina State University claims that the statistics cited above that show an 80 basis point difference between the cost of a variable annuity and a mutual fund ignore several important points. Huggard says that the SEC and a study by Arnott and Jeffrey in

1999 found that the typical mutual fund lost about 2.5 percent of its value each year to taxes and another 1 percent on average to commissions, raising the total annual costs to about 5 percent versus 2.2 percent on average for a variable annuity. His conclusion: In many cases, variable annuities are actually less expensive to own than mutual funds.

When comparing variable annuities, determine what other features are available such as online access, electronic funds transfer, dollar cost averaging, account rebalancing, number of transfers allowed per year, any transfer charges, flexibility of distribution options, and adequacy of account valuation statement.

Finally, depending on the annuity chosen, the choice of investment options may be limited or the presence of top performing fund managers may be absent. Investigate the number of sub-accounts and the range of investment options. Likewise, evaluate the fund performance in light of your investment goals and risk posture.

As baby boomers continue to move toward retirement age, look for them to have a growing interest in variable annuities as an excellent vehicle to fund their retirement dreams. Chart 17-1 illustrates the tax benefits of investing in a variable annuity versus a mutual fund. The early year results of the variable annuity are hampered by the deferred sales charge we have assumed in this example and the 10 percent tax penalty if the annuity is surrendered early. If you can stick it out for 10 years or more, the after-tax differences in favor of the variable annuity are potentially so huge that you cannot ignore them.

It is important to note that this illustration assumes that the entire annuity contract is liquidated at once, an unlikely event. If withdrawals are scattered over time, the comparison would favor the variable annuity even more over the mutual fund.

Einstein believed that compound interest was one of the great wonders of the world. Tax-deferred investing takes that one step beyond, putting all the dollars to work many times over instead of being diminished by the tax bite.

## Chart 17-1: Tax-Deferred Variable Annuity vs. Mutual Fund

TAX-DEFERRED VARIABLE ANNUITY CONTRACT

| Year | Age | Contract Value* | Deferred Sales Charge | Income Tax | Tax Penalty | Net After Taxes |
|---|---|---|---|---|---|---|
| 2002 | 59 | $100,000 | $7,000 | $0 | $0 | $93,000 |
| 2003 | 60 | $110,000 | $6,000 | $1,560 | $0 | $102,440 |
| 2004 | 61 | $121,000 | $5,000 | $6,240 | $0 | $109,760 |
| 2005 | 62 | $133,100 | $4,000 | $11,349 | $0 | $117,751 |
| 2006 | 63 | $146,410 | $3,000 | $16,930 | $0 | $126,480 |
| 2007 | 64 | $161,051 | $2,000 | $23,030 | $0 | $136,021 |
| 2008 | 65 | $177,156 | $1,000 | $29,701 | $0 | $146,455 |
| 2009 | 66 | $194,872 | $0 | $37,000 | $0 | $157,872 |
| 2010 | 67 | $214,359 | $0 | $44,600 | $0 | $169,759 |
| 2011 | 68 | $235,795 | $0 | $52,960 | $0 | $182,835 |
| 2012 | 69 | $259,374 | $0 | $62,156 | $0 | $197,218 |
| 2013 | 70 | $285,312 | $0 | $72,272 | $0 | $213,040 |
| 2014 | 71 | $313,843 | $0 | $83,399 | $0 | $230,444 |
| 2015 | 72 | $345,227 | $0 | $95,639 | $0 | $249,589 |
| 2016 | 73 | $379,750 | $0 | $109,102 | $0 | $270,647 |
| 2017 | 74 | $417,725 | $0 | $123,913 | $0 | $293,812 |
| 2018 | 75 | $459,497 | $0 | $140,204 | $0 | $319,293 |
| 2019 | 76 | $505,447 | $0 | $158,124 | $0 | $347,323 |
| 2020 | 77 | $555,992 | $0 | $177,837 | $0 | $378,155 |
| 2021 | 78 | $611,591 | $0 | $199,520 | $0 | $412,070 |
| 2022 | 79 | $672,750 | $0 | $223,372 | $0 | $449,377 |
| 2023 | 80 | $740,025 | $0 | $249,610 | $0 | $490,415 |
| 2024 | 81 | $814,027 | $0 | $278,471 | $0 | $535,557 |
| 2025 | 82 | $895,430 | $0 | $310,218 | $0 | $585,212 |
| 2026 | 83 | $984,973 | $0 | $345,140 | $0 | $639,834 |

*This assumes a 10.00% before-tax rate of return. A 39.00% marginal tax bracket is used.*

### MUTUAL FUND

| Year | Age | After Tax Fund Value | Deferred Sales Charge* | Net After Taxes | Net Difference In Favor Of Annuity |
|---|---|---|---|---|---|
| 2002 | 59 | $100,000 | $5,000 | $95,000 | ($2,000) |
| 2003 | 60 | $106,100 | $4,000 | $102,100 | $340 |
| 2004 | 61 | $112,572 | $3,000 | $109,572 | $188 |
| 2005 | 62 | $119,439 | $2,000 | $117,439 | $312 |
| 2006 | 63 | $126,725 | $1,000 | $125,725 | $755 |
| 2007 | 64 | $134,455 | $0 | $134,455 | $1,566 |
| 2008 | 65 | $142,657 | $0 | $142,657 | $3,798 |
| 2009 | 66 | $151,359 | $0 | $151,359 | $6,513 |
| 2010 | 67 | $160,592 | $0 | $160,592 | $9,167 |
| 2011 | 68 | $170,388 | $0 | $170,388 | $12,447 |
| 2012 | 69 | $180,781 | $0 | $180,781 | $16,437 |
| 2013 | 70 | $191,809 | $0 | $191,809 | $21,231 |
| 2014 | 71 | $203,509 | $0 | $203,509 | $26,935 |
| 2015 | 72 | $215,924 | $0 | $215,924 | $33,665 |
| 2016 | 73 | $229,095 | $0 | $229,095 | $41,553 |
| 2017 | 74 | $243,070 | $0 | $243,070 | $50,742 |
| 2018 | 75 | $257,897 | $0 | $257,897 | $61,396 |
| 2019 | 76 | $273,629 | $0 | $273,629 | $73,694 |
| 2020 | 77 | $290,320 | $0 | $290,320 | $87,835 |
| 2021 | 78 | $308,029 | $0 | $308,029 | $104,041 |
| 2022 | 79 | $326,819 | $0 | $326,819 | $122,558 |
| 2023 | 80 | $346,755 | $0 | $346,755 | $143,660 |
| 2024 | 81 | $367,907 | $0 | $367,907 | $167,649 |
| 2025 | 82 | $390,350 | $0 | $390,350 | $194,863 |
| 2026 | 83 | $414,161 | $0 | $414,161 | $225,673 |

*This assumes a 10.00% before-tax rate of return. A 39.00% marginal tax bracket is used.*

*If a no-load fund is used, the breakeven in favor of the annuity will take several years longer.*

*Courtesy of SIMCO*

Michael Henkel, president of Ibbotson Associates in Chicago, claims that annuities are an essential investment tool. "We are proponents of annuities if they're done intelligently." The real advantages of annuities are the tax-deferred growth and the promise of income checks for life, even if someone totally underestimates his or her life expectancy.

## A Word About Variable Universal Life Insurance

The simplest way I can describe variable universal life insurance (V.U.L.) is that it is a permanent life insurance policy allowing the owner of the policy to direct the cash value into and among the different investment options within the policy. In a traditional life policy, the insurance company sets and controls the rate of growth of cash value.

Some experts believe V.U.L. offers investors a better deal than traditional whole life insurance, but whether it is as cost effective as buying term insurance and investing the difference in a mutual fund or variable annuity is a matter of some debate. It appears to me that unless you can reasonably expect to earn 8-10 percent per year or more on the investment options within the policy and plan to hold it for at least 15 years or more, you should not choose to go the V.U.L. route. However, V.U.L. has become popular among some investors because if funded in at least four substantially equal payments over a seven year period, it allows investors to borrow tax-free, rather than withdraw from the policy. The loans are repaid before the cash value plus the remaining profits are paid tax-free to your heirs.

Maintaining a V.U.L. policy in compliance with all applicable regulations can be a complex task and should not be attempted without the guidance of an experienced life insurance expert. And, just as with a variable annuity contract, I do not believe that a

V.U.L. policy will reach its full potential without utilizing its equity investment options coupled with a
disciplined risk management strategy.

Fortunately, two large insurers, Prudential
(www.prudential.com) and John Hancock
(www.jhancock.com) have entered the V.U.L. market with products designed specifically to be coupled
with an active management strategy utilizing investment options from ProFunds and managed by a professional investment advisor.

## Key Points to Remember:

- Variable annuities can be excellent investments for certain people under the right
  circumstances.
- Variable annuities are an effective way to
  grow retirement assets efficiently while taking advantage of their tax-deferral benefits.
- Expanded death benefit features represent
  another attractive feature of variable annuities.
- Contrary to common belief, variable annuities
  provide a degree of security not afforded to
  owners of fixed annuities.
- A variety of variable annuity payout options
  gives investors the ability to plan their retirement income the way they want to receive it.
- One of the real advantages of annuities is the
  promise of income checks for life, even if
  someone totally underestimates his or her life
  expectancy.
- Before investing in variable annuities, be
  sure to read a prospectus and take into account all fees including the management fees,
  surrender charges, contract maintenance fee,

and an assessment to cover mortality and expense risk and administration.

· In certain cases, a variable universal life contract may also merit your consideration.

# MYTH #18

## This time it's different.

"Slump follows boom as night follows day. The good news is: boom follows slump as day follows night."

—*Colin Alexander*
*Timing The Stock Market*

"When you read contemporary accounts of booms and panics, the one thing that strikes you most forcibly is how little either stock speculation or stock speculators today differ from yesterday. The game does not change and neither does human nature."

—*Edwin Lefevre*
*Reminiscences of a Stock Operator (1923)*

### I Won't Say I Told You So, But . . .

In 1996, in my book, *Lasting Wealth Is A Matter Of Timing,* I warned: "I believe we received a warning shot across the Dow in 1987, one we should ignore only to the detriment of our financial well-being. That warning signal made me realize that simple asset allocation strategies and techniques will not save us from financial disaster during a full-blown bear market." And I devoted an entire section in Chapter 1 of that book to discussing "The Fallacy of 'It's Different This Time'." I said, "No, it is *not* different," and despite the high-tech euphoria of the time, I predicted that within the next five years that we could have another severe bear market decline.

Later, in 1999, I published a white paper detailing why I believed the Internet Revolution was a different, but not new, era! Here is a brief summary:

## The Internet Revolution . . . A Different, But Not New, Era!

After carefully analyzing the arguments of all of the "New Era" proponents that I could find, studying the markets and our econometric model back to 1927, and analyzing the forecasts of many leading economists, I have prepared the following summary (remember, this was in *1999*) of what I believe is the highest probability economic and market scenario for the not-too-distant future. I'm calling it a "different, but not new era," because we've seen it before, just not related to the Internet, but to other revolutionary technologies in the past, and not in the investing lifetime of most of today's market participants.

Some think that computers and the Internet are more important than the Industrial Revolution or even the invention of movable type printing, but they play the same role now that steel and chemicals did in the late 1800's and autos and electrification did in the 1920's. That is why I say it's a different, but not new, era.

Many of my conclusions dovetail with those of Dr. A. Gary Shilling, who I first met when we both

worked at Merrill Lynch in 1969, and who I acknowl-
edged in my book, *Lasting Wealth Is A Matter Of Timing*, as one of the persons most responsible for spark-
ing the ideas that formed the foundation of my investment philosophy. I believe that his book, *How To
Survive and Thrive In The Coming Wave Of Deflation*,
will become an investing classic.

After so many years of inflation, most Americans
do not believe that deflation is possible, and I have
had doubts myself. Most economists think that price
declines will be short-lived, largely confined to in-
ternationally traded commodities and are highly
unlikely to spread over the entire economy, especially the dominant service sector, which they see
as immune to foreign competition. Individual investors and consumers are even more convinced that
deflation is out of the question.

Nevertheless, what convinced me that deflation
may possibly be on the horizon is that 13 of the 14
deflationary forces that Shilling listed in his book
have already happened, and it is likely that the 14th
and last one, the conversion of U.S. consumers from
decades of borrowing and spending to many years of
saving, will be jump-started by a major bear market
in U.S. stocks that destroys a considerable part of
the portfolio appreciation that many Americans have
been using as a substitute for saving. This stock
sell-off will likely be triggered by disappointing U.S.
corporate profits or by a Federal Reserve-induced
recession if the American economy continues to boom
and to tighten labor markets.

Right now, U.S. stocks are vulnerable to disappointing earnings because they are so extremely overvalued. From the end of 1994 to the end of 1998, the
S&P 500 index rose 161 percent, but only one-third
of that came from higher earnings. Two-thirds re-

sulted from leaping price/earnings ratios (P/Es), which shoved stock prices to record levels. To a great extent, stocks have been celebrating the unwinding of inflation and making up for the beating they suffered during the inflationary late 1960's and 1970's. Nevertheless, many investors believe that what has really been a catch-up will continue indefinitely. There is an old Wall Street saying that stocks are driven by greed, tempered by fear. Even the 1987 crash and the 1990 and 1998 mini-crashes were only temporary interruptions. They were so quickly retraced that they have trained many investors to believe that sell-offs are wonderful opportunities to buy, not warnings to sell. That certainly was investor reaction to the market declines at the beginning of the Asian meltdown in the summer of 1997, the financial demise of Russia and crash of Long-Term Capital Management starting in August 1998, the Hong Kong crisis in October 1998, and the Brazilian devaluation in early 1999. Fear has been replaced by a conviction that the strong upward trend will last indefinitely, and by frustration if one is not fully invested in stocks. Confidence is rampant.

A final sign of a significant top in stock prices is the arrogance now prevalent among Wall Street brokers. A full-page *Wall Street Journal* ad by Paine Webber in 1998 said in screaming letters beneath a picture of a bear cave, "A Thought To Ponder As You Watch For The Bear To Emerge. YOU MAY BE IN FOR A VERY LONG WAIT."

I've learned, repeatedly, that when a majority believe that a market will continue to move in one direction indefinitely, a reversal is not too far away. The next bear market will probably be a Chinese water torture affair, with sell-offs met with buying that spawn weak rallies, followed by more sell-offs—

a long and frustrating saw-toothed pattern along a declining trend. As usual, even the true believers will ultimately dump their stocks, and thereby create the final bear market bottom.

## Time To Buy . . . Or Time To Sell?

On March 10, 2000, the exact day the NASDAQ peaked at 5,049 (it's now 1,114 as I write this in October, 2002), I sent a special "Caveat Emptor (Let the Buyer Beware)" bulletin to all of my investment management clients entitled, "Time To Buy . . . Or Time To Sell?" In that bulletin, I said, "Only time will tell, but when we look at the graph of the NASDAQ, the 5000 level doesn't look like an obvious buy point to us. It looks like Caveat Emptor (or Buyer Beware). That's why we are sending you this special bulletin today. We want to caution you about getting caught up in this market frenzy and taking unwarranted risks to your financial future. Be patient. We believe strongly that there will be another buying opportunity in tech stocks with much more favorable return/risk probabilities than are available today. In the meantime, Caveat Emptor!"

Obviously, the rest is history! I wasn't clairvoyant at the time. I was simply following the precepts of a prudent risk management investment strategy.

Jim Gipson, manager of the Clipper Fund, captured the essence of the market psychology prevailing in the late 1990's when he wrote:

**"Some professional hunters favor a lazy way to bag a lion. They leave fresh meat at the same spot each day and then blow a high-pitched whistle which lions can hear at great distance. Eventually the lions come to associate the whistle with dinner time. On**

the last day the professional hunter brings his client and then blows his whistle. The old lion comes expecting food but gets a bullet instead. What works for old lions in Africa probably will work for Young Lions on Wall Street, too. For years the stock market has only gone up with occasional small dips. Young Lions, who have no experience with any other kind of market, have been conditioned to buy on dips in anticipation of a coming rise in stock prices. Some day that conditioning, which has been helpful to date, will be fatal in the face of a long bear market which goes through the traditional four stages: 1. My stock is down a little. I'll buy more before it goes back up; 2. It's down even more, what a bargain! I'll spend my last cash reserves; 3. It can't go any lower. I'll hang on until I break even; 4. I can't stand it. Get me out now!"

Now let's move up to the present, October 2002. The Dow is down 36 percent from its high, the S&P 500 is down 48 percent, and the NASDAQ (remember, that's the market that would never go down) has dropped an astounding 78 percent. I'm starting to see some stage 4 behavior, "I can't stand it. Get me out now!" When does that typically occur? Answer: At or close to a major market bottom. This does not mean that you should run out and load up on stocks today. But it does mean that you should start making plans for the next bull market, not swearing off stocks for good like many are doing today. It definitely is not different this time. We were not headed to the moon in the market in 2000 any more than I believe that we are headed to zero today.

Looking at all of the stock market cycles since 1927, the duration of this bear market is now longer than 1973-74 and exceeded only by 1929-32. In loss percentages, it is again only rivaled by 1973-74 and two periods in the 1920's and 1930's. This means that both in time and in percentages, we should be fairly close to a bottom and the beginning of the next bull market.

Notice that I did not say the next "great" bull market. Unless prices drop significantly more from current levels, we will not likely have the dirt-cheap fundamental valuations that have set the stage for the truly great bull markets of the past. And there is always the possibility of a double-dip recession. The bull market of the 1990's was very much a "straight-up" affair; however, we expect that we might be heading into much more of a cyclical environment where an experienced active risk manager can become a much more important factor in your achieving investment success.

**"The four most expensive words in the English language are 'this time it's different'."**

**—*Attributed to Sir John Templeton***

## Key Points to Remember:

- It definitely is not different this time.
- When a majority believe that a market will continue to move in one direction indefinitely, a reversal is not too far away.
- It's profitable to be in stocks during bull markets, but it's even more profitable to be short stocks, or at least out of the market, during bear markets—even if many of the major bull market's months are completely missed.

# MYTH #19

## There is a "Holy Grail" in investing . . . I just need to find it!

"There is no Holy Grail or single indicator that can always forecast the market . . . and there never will be. However, by developing and following several time-proven indicators, a market analyst can answer a number of questions with surprising accuracy."

*—James B. Stack*
*Investech Research*

Sorry! There is no Holy Grail . . . no magic investment strategy or model or fund that will make you money every day, every month, or even every year. Benjamin Graham didn't have it (he lost over 70 percent of his clients' assets in 1929-32), Warren Buffett doesn't have it (he lost 23 percent in 1999, a year in which the S&P 500 was up in value over 20 percent, and more since then), and I don't have it. No one does!

No matter how good an investment model you have, it will have some periods where it overperforms its benchmark and others where it underperforms its benchmark.

The closest thing I know of to the "Holy Grail"

would be a portfolio consisting of multiple non-correlated active management strategies that would be automatically rebalanced for you at regular intervals.

Both Roger Schreiner at Select Advisors (1-800-351-0268, www.select-advisors.com) and Jerry Wagner of Flexible Plan Investments, Ltd. (1-800-347-3539, www.flexibleplan.com) have programs that can give you access to multiple non-correlated active management strategies, but the genius of Jerry Wagner is that he is the first manager to put it all together in a turnkey, suitability-driven format that he calls Allocation Plus™.

One of the reasons I joined forces with Jerry in 2001 was for me to be in a position to offer my clients strategies from more than one non-correlated model. I believe that Flexible Plan's Allocation Plus™ does this better than any other program from any other active money manager. In fact, Allocation Plus™ combines 30+ strategies from four different portfolio managers (four non-correlated models with more on the way) in a client suitability-driven program. You might have up to eight actively managed strategies in an account with as little as a $20,000 investment.

All you have to do is fill out a short Suitability Form that determines your risk profile and investment time horizon and say that you want to participate in Allocation Plus™. From that point on (once they have determined that you qualify, and you have signed the enrollment documents), everything is done automatically for you. For example, let's say your risk profile puts you in the Moderate Investor risk profile. Twenty or so of the strategies may be possible candidates for inclusion in your portfolio, but maybe only five to seven would be used at any one time—the ones that the Allocation Plus™ software selects as the best potential performers for the next quarter. During the quarter, each of the strategies is looked at each week and changes are made as called for by the respective strategies. Once a quarter, Allocation Plus™ itself is rebalanced, with strategies automatically added and deleted and percentages changed as necessary for optimizing performance potential.

And here's what really impresses me—hypothetical computer simulations have shown that using these non-correlated models with automatic rebalancing reduces risk without sacrificing return potential, and the actual returns since inception earlier this year reinforce this observation.

## Chart 19-1: Strategic Solutions Allocation Plus™ Research Report

### Capital Market Line Analysis (Hypothetical) 1994-2001*

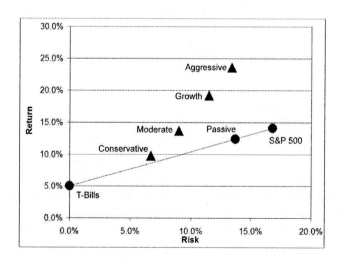

|             | S&P 500 | Passive | Aggressive* | Growth* | Moderate* | Conservative* |
|-------------|---------|---------|-------------|---------|-----------|---------------|
| Return      | 14.10%  | 12.40%  | 23.60%      | 19.20%  | 13.70%    | 9.80%         |
| Risk        | 16.80%  | 13.70%  | 13.40%      | 11.50%  | 9.00%     | 6.70%         |
| Risk-Adj Ret| 0.54    | 0.54    | 1.38        | 1.23    | 0.96      | 0.72          |
| Beta        | 1       | 0.75    | 0.52        | 0.49    | 0.41      | 0.31          |
| Alpha       | 0.00%   | 0.60%   | 13.90%      | 9.70%   | 5.00%     | 2.00%         |
| Max. Loss   | -35.70% | -26.80% | -11.20%     | -7.40%  | -8.20%    | -7.90%        |
| *Hypothetical after maximum fees.* |

*S&P 500=Standard and Poors 500 Index*
*Passive=Returns of buying and holding an equal dollar investment in each of the*
*funds available for Allocation Plus™*
*Aggressive, Growth, Moderate, Conservative=Returns over the period utilizing the*
*suitability profile listed in the column heading*
*Courtesy of Flexible Plan Investments, Ltd.*
*See Appendix E for Disclosure Statement*

Strategic Solutions Allocation Plus™
Actual Results
6 months ending 9/30/2002
(After maximum fees*)

|                           | Return  | Risk**  |
|---------------------------|---------|---------|
| Conservative              | -4.20%  | 3.90%   |
| Moderate                  | -6.20%  | 3.80%   |
| Growth                    | -12.20% | 6.00%   |
| Aggressive                | -14.20% | 6.20%   |
| Dow Jones Industrial Average | -27.00% | 14.00% |
| S&P 500                   | -28.40% | 14.00%  |
| NASDAQ                    | -36.50% | 11.90%  |

*Courtesy of Flexible Plan Investments, Ltd.*
*See Appendix D for Disclosure Statement*
*\* Not inclusive of 1.2% establishment fee*
*\*\* Risk=Standard Deviation*

Some might say that the actual results shown above are not that impressive since they show negative results for the first full six months of actual trading. In response, I would point out that the mathematics of investing greatly favor any strategy that can significantly reduce drawdowns during adverse market periods as Allocation Plus™ has done.

For example, if you lose 50 percent, you have to make 100 percent on what you have left just to get back to breakeven. And if you lost 70 percent as Benjamin Graham did for his clients in 1929-32, you would have to make 233 percent just to get back to breakeven. On the other hand, I am sure that you can see that an investment program like Allocation Plus™, whose losses were only 4 percent to 14 percent when the major indices were down 27 percent to 36 percent, has a big advantage in helping you achieve your investment goals. It is not the Holy Grail, but it may offer you the highest probability of becoming wealthy while keeping your investment risk at a suitable level.

## Key Points to Remember:

· There is no Holy Grail in investing!
· The mathematics of gains and losses favors investment programs that reduce drawdowns in account values during bear markets.
· Using multiple non-correlated investment strategies may give you the highest probability of achieving your investment goals.
· Flexible Plan Investments' Allocation Plus™ is the current market leader in this field.

# Epilogue

## Summarizing the Alternatives

I trust that I have made a solid case in this book for the importance of maintaining a healthy percentage of your investment assets committed to equities, even during your golden years of retirement. If this concept needs to be reinforced, refer back to the tale of Connie Conservative in Myth #4.

With regard to stock market investing, I have tried to show you that the individual investor basically has four alternatives:

1. Buy and Hold Investing—Has theoretically provided enough return to offset taxes and inflation, but very few investors have the emotional strength to ride out all the ups and downs of the stock market. As we showed with Peter Hope in Myth #11, this strategy can literally wipe you out if a bear market occurs after you retire and are making regular withdrawals.

2. Dollar Cost Averaging—Can be a valuable tool for disciplining a young person to save and invest regularly. However, it does *not* offer protection against bear markets and; therefore, it is a dangerous and risky strategy in a mature portfolio, unless coupled with active risk management.

3. Passive Asset Allocation—Can provide some reduction in risk by spreading your portfolio among a variety of different asset classes, but also sacrifices significant return potential in the process. Furthermore, the risk protection aspect of passive (strategic) asset allocation is highly overrated. After all, 60 percent of a 50 percent bear market decline is still a 30 percent loss, higher than many investors can stomach.

4. Active Risk Management—Has historically kept bear market losses low enough to keep investors committed to equities and, as a by-product, given investors a superior risk-adjusted return. I believe that it is the only one of the four alternatives that is likely to save our generation and future generations from irreparable financial damage over the long term.

Obviously, I believe that active risk management is the best strategy you can use to reduce the risks of stock market investing. Yet, I realize that some of you may have read elsewhere that it does not work, that no one can successfully beat buy and hold investing over the long haul. The contradiction may be confusing, and you may feel that you still do not know what to do!

I offer this suggestion. When I have found myself in a similar dilemma, I found it helpful to list each possible outcome and the likely end result for me personally. Let's go through this exercise with active risk management and see if it benefits you.

| Possible Outcomes | Likely End Results |
|---|---|
| 1. Active risk management works/you use it. | Great, you will probably become rich. |
| 2. Active risk management does not work/you use it. | You will make less return than if you did not use it; however, your risk should also be lowered. |
| 3. Active risk management does not work/you don't use it. | So what! |
| 4. Active risk management works/you don't use it. | You may be completely wiped out, especially if you have to make withdrawals during a prolonged bear market. |

What option will you choose to take? My bet is that you are thinking that you would be nuts not to use a disciplined risk management strategy. It is a pure case of reward versus risk. Compare the end results. The worst case scenario while using active risk management (2.) means you might earn less return. On the other extreme, the worst case of not using active risk management (4.) could mean you end up flat broke. You do not have to be a genius to conclude that you need to find a good professional risk management advisor today.

If you made it this far in the book, congratulations! You are a winner, because you are now one of those special people who has debunked the myths and now can say, "Everything I Know About Investing Is Right!"

# Appendix A

## Disclosure Statement

### Summary

The active risk management model is based on a set of proprietary indicators and calculations used to project major market movements. This model was originated by John K. Sosnowy in 1970. The model is used to determine when to change the allocations in, and/or exchange into and out of various funds having different investment objectives within families of mutual funds.

We are committed to state-of-the-art applications of modern portfolio theory utilizing historical simulation techniques. As a result of this ongoing quantitative research, modifications and improvements have been made to the model over the years and are expected to be made in the future. We believe it is not only important for a client or potential client to know the actual results that our model existing at the time generated, but also the results that the model as currently formulated would have generated. We have historical data on the key variables in our model all the way back to 1927. Therefore, we can and do run computer simulations back-testing today's model as far back as 1927. This gives us a much greater comfort level about the decisions we made for model improvements than if we based them only on data back to 1970.

## Parameters

The results of "buy" and "sell" signals generated by today's model are shown in the illustrations, in relation to the movement of the specific portfolios and/or indices utilized. *These illustrations are hypothetical and do not represent actual trading using client assets.*

These illustrations are net of all charges, expenses and fees, and assume the reinvestment of all dividends and capital gains. Nothing has been taken out for taxes. Money Market funds were not widely available prior to 1975; therefore, we use short-term T-Bills as our money market investment on any illustration going back prior to 1975. All prices are the weekly close nearest to the actual exchange date. The stock, bond, and money market portfolios used in this illustration are not necessarily from the same fund family, as would normally be the case in an actual account.

The NYSE TR Index represents all stocks on the New York Stock Exchange, with dividends reinvested. It is an unmanaged index. You cannot actually invest in the NYSE TR Index. Since 3/31/2000, the change in the Wilshire 5000 Total Market Index has been used as the best proxy for the change in the NYSE TR Index, since NYSE TR data is no longer available from its historical source and the Wilshire 5000 is generally regarded as the best measure of the entire U. S. stock market today. The Wilshire 5000 Total Market Index measures the performance of all U. S. headquartered equity securities with readily available price data. It is an unmanaged index. You cannot actually invest in the Wilshire 5000 Index.

## Limitations

*There are limitations inherent in running historical simulations. Back tested performance is not as accurate and dependable a measure of profitability as actual trading results because it is achieved by means of the retroactive application of a model that is designed with the benefit of hindsight. Some slippage in return is to be expected as you move from research to actual practice. Back tested performance also may not reflect the impact that any material market or economic factors might have had on the use of the model if today's had actually been used during the period to manage client assets.* We minimize this potential impact and take the emotions out of the equation by utilizing a purely quantitative system with disciplined implementation procedures. And by performing diligent in-sample period testing along with out-of-sample period confirmation, we build a robust model with the best possible opportunity of real-time success.

## Risks

*The volatility of the portfolios and/or indices used in these illustrations may be materially different from the mutual fund and/or annuity portfolio actually utilized by a client. Additionally, the portfolio composition of the funds used by clients having similar investment objectives may materially differ from each other as well as the portfolios used in this illustration. Therefore, the results which could be obtained by an investor could be materially different from the results portrayed here and the actual results of clients depending*

*on the performance of the particular investments
chosen by him and the costs and expenses associated with such investments.* The investment return
and principal value of an investment will fluctuate
so that an investor's shares, when received, may be
worth more or less than their original cost. Also, an
investment using variable annuity contracts will involve additional expenses and limitations.

Market volatility can significantly impact short-
term results. Results of an investment made today
may differ substantially from the back tested numbers shown. The data quoted represents model research, which may have benefited from a period of
generally rising prices. *Past model research results
should in no way be construed as a guarantee of
future return.*

# Appendix B

## Disclosure Statement

"Model Account" results for the identified invest-ment management strategy shown are time-weighted, monthly, geometrically linked returns, and to facili-tate timely month-end reporting, are from single re-viewed client accounts as representative of returns which reflect actual fund families and reflect the actual dates of Flexible Plan's buy and sell signals. If an account terminates during a period, an alter-native single account is substituted. Selection of accounts is based on longevity and least amount of additions and withdrawals.

While our original methodologies continue to be used, enhancements have been made on several oc-casions. It is believed these have had a positive im-pact on returns, the extent of which is not precisely quantifiable. Efforts to develop indicators are ongo-ing and may result in further changes. Dividends are reinvested. Mutual fund or annuity results will vary based upon their volatility as they relate to the S&P 500 Index or other indices that may be used as a benchmark. Specific mutual funds, sub-accounts or indices may materially outperform or underperform these results. Various mutual funds or sub-accounts used in any model account may no longer be avail-able due to fund consolidations and exchange conditions imposed by the funds or annuity. Inclusion of an index is demonstrative only. No index is a directly tradable investment.

Evolution™ fees are deducted quarterly at the rate of 1.8% annually. Minimum account size $100,000. Actual fees will vary between 1.0% and 1.8% annually. All mutual fund management fees are included; other non-advisory plan administrative fees are not. Review the fund or annuity prospectus for additional information. If a load fund purchase is contemplated, any commission charged should be deducted. As individual tax rates vary, taxes have not been considered.

***Past performance does not guarantee future results.***

# Appendix C

## Disclosure Statement

### Summary

The active risk management model is based on a set of proprietary indicators and calculations used to project major market movements. This model was originated by John K. Sosnowy in 1970. The model is used to determine when to change the allocations in, and/or exchange into and out of various funds having different investment objectives within families of mutual funds.

### Parameters

The results of actual "buy" and "sell" signals generated by the model are shown in the following illustrations in relation to the movement of the specific portfolios and/or indices utilized. *These results would have to be considered hypothetical because they use actual switching signals, but not actual client account performance and therefore, the results DO NOT represent actual trading or the experience of any client during the periods shown, nor do they reflect the impact on decision-making of economic or market factors experienced during actual management of funds.* It should also be noted that actual account records prior to 1979 are not available even though switching signal dates are available back to 1970. Sosnowy and his former partner issued a joint sell recommendation in conflict with the model on 11/10/82; however, steps have been taken to insure that such recommendations in conflict with the model will not be issued in the future.

These illustrations are net of all charges, expenses and fees, and assume the reinvestment of all dividends and capital gains. Nothing has been taken out for taxes. Money Market funds were not widely available prior to 1975; therefore, we use short-term T-Bills as our money market investment on any illustration going back prior to 1975. All prices are the weekly close nearest to the actual exchange date. The stock, bond, and money market portfolios used in this illustration are not necessarily from the same fund family, as would normally be the case in an actual account.

The NYSE TR Index represents all stocks on the New York Stock Exchange, with dividends reinvested. It is an unmanaged index. You cannot actually invest in the NYSE TR Index. Since 3/31/2000, the change in the Wilshire 5000 Total Market Index has been used as the best proxy for the change in the NYSE TR Index, since NYSE TR data is no longer available from its historical source and the Wilshire 5000 is generally regarded as the best measure of the entire U. S. stock market today. The Wilshire 5000 Total Market Index measures the performance of all U. S. headquartered equity securities with readily available price data. It is an unmanaged index. You cannot actually invest in the Wilshire 5000 Index.

## Risks

The volatility of the portfolios and/or indices used in these illustrations may be materially different from the mutual fund and/or annuity portfolio actually utilized by a client. Additionally, the portfolio composition of the funds used by clients having similar investment objectives may materially differ from each other as well as the portfolios used in this illustration. Therefore, the actual results that could be obtained by an investor would, of course, vary depending on the performance of the particular investments chosen by him and the costs and expenses associated with such investments. The investment return and principal value of an investment will fluctuate so that an investor's shares, when received, may be worth more or less than their original cost. Also, an investment using variable annuity contracts will involve additional expenses and limitations.

Market volatility can significantly impact short-term returns. Results of an investment made today may differ substantially from the numbers shown in this illustration. The data quoted represents model results, which may have benefited from a period of generally rising prices. *Past model results presented here should in no way be construed as a guarantee of future return.*

# Appendix D

## Disclosure Statement

### Flexible Plan Investments, Ltd.
### "Model Account" Rate of Return Report (After Fees)

"Model Account" results for the identified investment management strategy shown are time-weighted, monthly, geometrically linked returns. Except for the Market SAVI model results (M—SAVI), to facilitate timely month-end reporting, "Model Accounts" are from single reviewed accounts as representative returns, which reflect actual fund families and reflect the actual dates of Flexible Plan's buy and sell signals. If an account terminates during a period, an alternative single account is substituted. Selection of accounts is based on longevity and least amount of additions and withdrawals. Since M—SAVI accounts are typically combinations of strategies, and because varying start dates and consequent rebalancing affects account returns, M—SAVI results where noted do not represent the actual experience of any client during the period. Noted M—SAVI results are derived using actual trade history to determine the weekly strategy positions and are rebalanced on a weekly basis unlike an individual client account that might only trade 100% from one fund to another without rebalancing during the trading week. The effect of applying this methodology is not precisely quantifiable; results may tend to be understated as compared to the market direction.

Enhancements have been made in several of our methodologies on numerous occasions. It is believed that these have had a positive effect on returns, the extent of which is not precisely quantifiable. In August 2001, indicators developed and maintained by John Sosnowy, whose business was acquired by Flexible Plan in 2001, replaced indicators used in Classic. Mr. Sosnowy continues to maintain these indicators as an employee. Therefore, the performance results reflect the results of the Classic strategy indicators as applied prior to August 2001, and the results of the Sosnowy indicators thereafter. Efforts to develop indicators are ongoing and may result in further changes. Dividends are reinvested. Mutual fund or annuity results will vary based upon their volatility as they relate to the S&P 500 Index or other indices that may be used as a benchmark. Specific mutual funds, sub-accounts or indices may materially outperform or underperform these results. Various mutual funds or sub-accounts used in any model account may no longer be available due to fund consolidations and exchange conditions imposed by the funds or annuity. Inclusion of an index is demonstrative only. No index is a directly tradable investment. As individual tax rates vary, taxes have not been considered.

Evolution™ fees are deducted quarterly at the rate of 1.8% annually (minimum $100,000 account). Actual fees will vary between 1.0% and 2.6% annually. Prior to 31 December 1995, Classic fees are deducted quarterly at the rate of 2.8% annually and at 2.6% thereafter. Effective 1 January 1996, actual fees will vary between .9 and 2.6% annually, depending on assets under management, and are billed quarterly. Strategic Solutions and Market SAVI fees are deducted quarterly at the rate of 2.6% annually. Actual fees will vary between 1.0% and 2.6% annually. The maximum Strategic Solutions Establishment Fee is 1.2%. All mutual fund fees and expenses are included to the extent they are reflected in net asset value; other fees may apply. If a load fund purchase is contemplated, any commission charged should be deducted.

### *Past performance does not guarantee future results.*

*Performance for the period, generally encompassing 1999 and the first quarter of 2000 was driven by substantial price appreciation in a small number of equity issues, notably in technology sectors, traded primarily on the NASDAQ. Such performance is historical information and should not be relied upon as representative of investment performance of any strategy to the current date nor be extrapolated into expectations for the future. Inquiry for current results is advised, in light of the adverse market performance of many indices commencing in 2000. Inherent in any investment is the potential for loss as well as the potential for gain. A list of all recommendations made within the immediately preceding year is available upon written request.*

# Appendix E

## Disclosure Statement

The Research Report results are HYPOTHETICAL. See "Appendix E Definitions" for explanation of testing methodologies. The performance results depicted have been produced by application of selected mathematical calculation criteria to historical price data. Results DO NOT represent actual trading or the experience of any client during the periods shown, nor do they reflect the impact on decision-making of economic or market factors experienced during actual management of funds.

Advisory fees vary between 1% to 2.6% yearly dependent on assets under management. The maximum percentage is prorated and deducted quarterly. Expenses of the funds are included to the extent they are reflected in the NAV. Other fees may apply. The maximum Establishment fee of 1.2% has been deducted from the initial balance. Distributions have been invested. As individual tax rates vary, taxes have not been considered.

No index is directly tradable. Actual investment performance of any trading strategy may frequently be materially different than the results shown. Some funds used in the model may not be available for future use. As supplemental information, a listing of all assumed trades and other data used to generate the referenced results is available upon request.

## *Past performance does not guarantee future results.*

Performance for the period, generally encompassing 1999 and the first quarter of 2000, as shown in
both actual accounts and results of hypothetical testing, was driven by substantial price appreciation in
a relatively small number of equity issues, notably
in various technology sectors, traded primarily on
the NASDAQ. Such performance is historical information and should not be relied upon as necessarily
representative of investment performance of any
strategy to the current date nor be extrapolated into
expectations for the future. Inquiry for more current
results is advised, particularly in light of the adverse market performance of many indices for the
period commencing in the second quarter of the year
2000 and continuing into 2001. Inherent in any investment is the potential for loss as well as the potential for gain. A list of all recommendations made
within the immediately preceding year is available
upon written request.

## Appendix E Definitions:

Capital Market Line (CML): CML graphically depicts the
relationship between risk (as measured by volatility using
the investment's Standard Deviation) and Compounded
Annual Rate of Return. By plotting the risk and return (hori-
zontal and vertical axes, respectively) of an investment on
a chart, one can compare such measurements to the same
qualities of a Benchmark (e.g., the S&P 500). The line drawn
between the T-Bill Rate of Return and the Benchmark is
known as the Capital Market Line (CML). Values above the
line represent a level of return greater than historical data

would predict for the level of risk exhibited by the investment. Values below the line demonstrate lower than expected returns.

Risk (Standard Deviation): Standard Deviation is a statistical measurement of the dispersion or variability of the return of a security from the mean average. It is one measure of volatility. In the case of mutual funds, it depicts how widely weekly returns varied over a certain period of time. Standard Deviation uses the volatility of an investment's historical returns to predict the most likely range of its future returns. When a fund has a high standard deviation, this predicted range is wide, implying greater volatility and, therefore, a greater level of risk. Investors are cautioned, however, that in calculating risk, high positive returns are treated the same as high negative returns. Thus, strategies with above-average returns can have high standard deviations. See "Special Risk Consideration" in Brochure Form ADV, available upon request from Flexible Plan Investments, Ltd.

Beta: Beta is a measurement of the risk of a security as determined from its sensitivity to market movements. Beta is obtained by measuring the variability of weekly returns as compared to a "benchmark" market measure (e.g., the S&P 500). The beta of the benchmark is "1" by definition. The beta for US T-Bills is "0". Low or even negative betas may also be indicative of low correlation of return with the benchmark, i.e., different risk characteristics are being exhibited between the research portfolio and the benchmark. Thus, the lower the beta of an investment the less volatile or risky that measurement is when compared to the benchmark. Conversely, a beta higher than "1" implies greater volatility than the benchmark market index.

Alpha: Alpha is a measurement of the risk-adjusted rate of return of a security. The alpha of the benchmark (e.g., the S&P 500) is always equal to zero. Given its level of risk, alpha measures the difference between a fund's actual weekly return and its expected return for the level of risk the fund has exhibited historically. Risk is measured by beta. A positive alpha indicates the fund has actually performed better than its beta would predict. A negative alpha indicates the fund's underperformance, given the risk expectations established by the fund's beta. Each of the previously described statistics is annualized for easy comparison.

Maximum Loss: The percentage drop from the highest weekly level of equity to the subsequent lowest level. Also referred to as maximum drawdown.

Risk-adjusted Return: The Risk-adjusted Return determines the reward per unit of risk. The higher the value, the better the fund's historical risk-adjusted performance. It is calculated by dividing a fund's annualized excess returns (return — 90-day T-Bill) by the standard deviation of a fund's annualized returns. Also referred to as the Sharpe Ratio.

Return: Return is the Compounded Annual Return for the time periods shown. Annual returns are compounded weekly and are inclusive of the last full trading week of the year, but may not necessarily include the last trading day of the year. Fees have been subtracted.

Efficient Frontier: Graphically represents a set of portfolio diversifications which maximize expected returns for each level of risk. Simply stated, find a comfortable level of risk and move upward to locate the portfolio which corresponds to that risk. The selected portfolio seeks to produce the maximum return for the level of risk preferred. The combination of the best portfolios for a given level of risk produces the Efficient Frontier.

"Walk-forward" Testing: The results of this research report were not generated from an optimization procedure, rather, a method known as "walk-forward testing" was used. This ensures that we do not use information which would not have been available to us at the time. For example, to test the year 1993, we only used data which was available at the end of 1992. The same thing was done for each of the subsequent years. Of course, this method does not ensure that the future will mirror the past, but it does give us the confidence that our strategies are robust enough to be effective going forward in time.

Passive: Results shown for a Passive investment represent the risks and returns of an equal dollar investment in each of the funds that were in the Fund Universe from which funds could be chosen by the strategy described. As such, we believe they are representative of the market and economic conditions during the periods shown. However, we also believe it is unlikely that any investor would own equal dollar investments in every fund in the fund universe.

Minimum or Maximum Fees: Results are shown after Minimum Fees (1%) or Maximum Fees (2.6%) to illustrate the performance for the full range of fees charged. The Maximum Fees for Strategic Solutions results also include the full establishment fee of 1.2%. These fees are not taken into account in computing Risk, Beta, Alpha, Risk-Adjusted Return or Maximum Loss.

Dollar Growth: Shows the 5- and 10-year growth of the initial investment if invested at the S&P 500, Passive, and Combination's rates of return as calculated over the previous 8 years. The establishment fee, if chosen, is deducted, as are management fees based on initial account size. Inclusion of this calculation is not meant to imply that such returns will be achieved. It is merely meant to illustrate the power of compounding at the rate determined by the research for the account size chosen.

In-Sample and Out-of-Sample: In-sample testing used on some of the tactical asset allocation strategies refers to the optimization of system parameters for a limited period of the total test period available. Out-of-sample testing means taking the optimized parameters from the in-sample test period and applying them to dates not used in such optimizations.

# Glossary

**Active Asset Allocation.** An asset allocation strategy involving continuous monitoring and periodic rebalancing of the portfolio as needed among multiple asset classifications, usually done in increments. See also dynamic asset allocation.

**Active Risk Management.** An investment strategy designed to reduce the exposure to market risk when the probability of loss is high. See also, active, dynamic, and tactical asset allocation, and market timing.

**Alpha.** The difference between portfolio return and expected return. A positive alpha means a portfolio has earned a premium over what is expected given the level of risk-free return, market index return, and the volatility of the portfolio as expressed by beta.

**Annual Report.** The Securities and Exchange Commission required report presenting a portrayal of the company's operations and financial position. It includes a balance sheet, income statement, statement of cash flows, description of company operations, management discussion of company financial condition and operating results, and any events which materially impact the company.

**Annuity.** A series of payments continuing until death. An annuity contract, issued by an insurance company, provides a series of payments for the life of the annuitant or for an agreed-upon number of years. See also Fixed Annuity and Variable Annuity.

**Artificial Intelligence.** The field of computer science dedicated to producing software that attempts to mimic the processes of the human brain.

**Asset Allocation.** Investment strategy of reducing risk and increasing return potential by investing in a variety of asset types. Also known as strategic or passive allocation because changes in allocation are made very infrequently.

**Back End Load.** A sales charge that is only deducted at redemption of fund shares. The charge typically decreases to zero over time. Also known as deferred sales charge.

**Back-Testing.** An important tool in model building. A strategy is tested on historical data, and then the strategy is applied to new, or out-of-sample data to determine whether the results are consistent with the sample.

**Basis Point.** Gradation of fixed income yields based on a 100-point scale representing one percent. For example, the yield difference between 7.75 percent and 7.95 percent is 20 basis points.

**Bear Market.** A period of time during which stock prices decline over a period of months or years. It is usually defined by a fall in prices in excess of 20 percent on the major benchmark indices.

**Beta.** A measure of volatility comparing the returns of an individual investment relative to the market. Securities with a beta of 1.0 are equal in risk to that of the overall market. Stocks with betas greater than 1.0 possess more risk than the market while stocks with betas less than 1.0 have less risk than the market.

**Bond.** A long-term debt security which obligates the issuer to pay interest and repay the principal. The holder does not have any ownership rights in the issuer.

**Bottom Up Investing.** Investment strategy starting with company fundamentals and then moving to the overall economic and investment environment.

**Bull Market.** A period of time during which stock prices advance over a period of months or years. It is usually defined by a rise in prices in excess of 25 percent on the major benchmark indices.

**Buy and Hold.** A strategy of purchasing a portfolio of securities and riding out all of the ups and downs of the market over the long-term.

**Call Option.** A contract providing the holder the right to buy the underlying security at a specific price for a specified time period.

**Capital Gains.** The profits received and distributed from the sale of securities within the portfolio.

**Capitalization Weighted Index.** A market average such as the S&P 500 that takes into account the market value of each security in the index.

**Cash Equivalent.** An asset type with maturities of less than one year. Also known as a money market security.

**Closed-End Fund.** An investment fund with a fixed number of shares outstanding and trades on exchanges like stock in regular companies.

**Contrarian.** An investor seeking securities out-of-favor with other investors.

**Correction.** A price decline with the market retracting some of its previous gains, but not enough to be defined as a bear market.

**Cost-Benefit Analysis.** A review of the incremental costs and benefits associated with a specific trading strategy.

**Covered Call.** An option in which the investor owns the underlying security.

**Cross-Correlation.** Analysis of investment returns of different asset classes to determine whether or not they move in conjunction with or counter to other asset classifications.

**Cycles.** Repeating patterns of business, economic and market activity. The length of a cycle is measured in trading days from bottom to bottom. The end of one cycle is the beginning of the next. See also market cycle.

**Cyclical.** Industries and companies that advance and decline in relation to the changes in the overall economic environment.

**Day.** A trading day, weekends and holidays excluded.

**Defensive Investments.** Securities that are less affected by economic contractions, thus offering some downside price protection.

**Discount Rate.** The interest rate the Federal Reserve charges on loans to member banks.

**Discretionary Account.** An account in which trades are effected without prior client approval, usually through the use of a limited power of attorney.

**Diversification.** The spreading of investment risk by owning different types of securities, investments in different geographical markets, etc.

**Dollar Cost Averaging.** Investment strategy of investing a fixed amount of money over time to achieve a lower average security purchase price.

**Dow Jones Industrial Average.** Market index consisting of 30 U.S. industrial companies. Used as a measure of market performance.

**Dow Theory.** Investment theory that the market moves in three simultaneous movements, which help forecast the direction of the economy and the market.

**Drawdown.** The reduction in account equity (or value) as a result of a trade or series of trades over a defined period of time. Maximum drawdown can be best expressed as the worst paper loss over the period.

**Dynamic Asset Allocation.** An asset allocation strategy involving continuous monitoring and periodic rebalancing of the portfolio as needed among multiple asset classifications based on an analysis of the current reward/risk ratio in each class as well as changes in investor circumstances. Rebalancing is usually done in increments. See also active asset allocation.

**Earnings Per Share.** Net after-tax income divided by the number of outstanding company shares.

**Economic Series.** The complete cycle of economic periods such as from expansion to slowdown to contraction to recession/depression to increased activity back to expansion.

**Efficient Market.** A market that instantly takes into account all known financial information and reflects it in the security's price.

**Emerging Markets.** Securities markets in countries other than those, such as the United States, England, Germany, Japan, etc., which are considered to be established, developed markets.

**Exercise Price.** The price at which an option of futures contract can be executed. Also known as the striking price.

**Expected Return.** The return one should have expected given the risk taken, overall market returns, and the level of risk-free returns.

**Expected Value.** An anticipated value of a strategy based on probability.

**Expert System.** A rule-driven artificial intelligence trading system requiring an expert to interpret the indicators. An expert system possesses the advantage of being able to outperform many mechanical systems.

**Expiration Date.** The last day on which an option or future can be exercised.

**Fed.** Short for Federal Reserve.

**Federal Funds.** Also known as Fed Funds. They are the legal reserves required to be held by banks and often borrowed and lent between banks overnight. The interest rate charged on Fed Funds is known as the Fed Funds Rate.

**Federal Reserve.** The national banking system consisting of 12 independent federal reserve banks in Atlanta, Boston, Chicago, Cleveland, Dallas, Kansas City, Minneapolis, New York, Philadelphia, Richmond, St. Louis and San Francisco.

**Financial Intermediary.** A financial institution such as a trust company or an investment manager who directs other people's money into investments.

**Financial Planner.** One who prepares investment, tax, estate, and/or insurance plans and may provide advice as to the implementation of such plans.

**Fiscal Year.** The 12-month accounting period that conforms to the company's natural operating cycle versus the calendar year.

**Fixed Annuity.** A contract issued by an insurance company guaranteeing a particular rate of interest for a certain period of time, after which the guaranteed rate is reset.

**Forecasting.** Making projections about the future direction of the economy and the markets, usually based on fundamental analysis.

**Formula Investing.** An investment strategy that shifts portfolio assets from one asset classification to another based on predetermined factors.

**401(k) Plan.** A defined contribution retirement plan that allows employees to contribute part of their salary before taxes. Many plans offer a variety of investment options, including stock, bond and money market funds.

**Front End Load.** A mutual fund sold to the public at the offering price. The difference between the offering price and net asset value represents a sales charge on each investment in the fund.

**Fundamental Analysis.** Investment strategy focusing on the intrinsic value of the company as evidenced by a review of the balance sheet, income statement, cash flow and operating performance. Can also be applied to the market as a whole.

**Fund Timing.** Moving in and out of stock funds based on a technical signal, often based on the price of the fund moving above or below a moving average. Also known as fund conversion or fund switching.

**Gap.** A trading pattern when the price range from one day does not overlap the previous day's price range.

**Growth Investments.** Companies or industries with earnings projected to outpace the market consistently over the long-term.

**Hedging.** The use of derivative securities such as options or futures in an attempt to reduce or eliminate the risk of holding another security.

**High-Tech Stock.** Securities of firms in high-technology industries such as biotechnology, computers, electronics, lasers, medical devices and robotics.

**High Yield Bond.** Also known as a junk bond.

**Hybrid Security.** A security that possesses the characteristics of both a stock and a bond, such as a convertible bond.

**Index.** Compilation of performance for specific groupings of stocks or mutual funds such as the Dow Jones Industrial Average and S&P 500.

**Index Fund.** A mutual fund whose objective is to mirror the performance of a popular index such as the S&P 500.

**Index Option.** An option on a specific market index such as the S&P 100 (OEX). Also known as a cash settlement option.

**Indicator.** A measurement of the economy or securities markets used by economists and investment analysts to predict future economic and financial moves and direction. Indicators are classified as leading, coincidental or lagging. This can be based on fundamental, monetary, sentiment, or momentum factors. Indicator examples include interest rate changes, price-to-earnings ratios, and number of unemployment claims, etc.

**Individual Retirement Account (IRA).** A tax-deferred retirement account for wage earners. An IRA account holder must begin taking distributions by April 1 of the year after reaching age 70 1/2.

**Inflation.** A general rise in the prices of goods and services. The Consumer Price Index and the Producer Price Index are two measures of inflation.

**IPO (Initial Public Offering).** The first public offering of a company's stock.

**Insider.** Anyone having access to material corporate information. Most frequently used to refer to company officers, directors and top management.

**Institutional Investor.** Investor organizations, such as pension funds and money managers, which trade large volumes of securities.

**In The Money.** The situation when the price of the underlying security is above the exercise price.

**Internal Rate Of Return.** Also known as Dollar Weighted Return; so called because it gives greater weight to those time periods when more money was invested. Not suitable for determining the relative skill of a manager.

**Intrinsic Value.** The difference between the current market price of the underlying security and the striking price of a related option.

**Inverse Fund.** A mutual fund whose investment results are designed to inversely correlate with a major market average such as the S&P 500.

**Investment Manager.** One acting as an investment advisor to other people. The arrangement may or may not involve discretionary authority to make trades on behalf of the client. See also registered investment advisor.

**Investment Style.** The predominant investment philosophy of an investment manager, such as a value investor, momentum player, earnings driven, market timer, etc.

**Junk Bond.** A bond with ratings below investment grade.

**Leading Indicator.** An economic measurement that tends to accurately predict the future direction of the economy or stock market.

**LEAPS.** Long-term equity participation securities. Long-term options with maturities up to two years.

**Life Cycle Investing.** Developing an investment strategy based on where you are in your life cycle.

**Liquidity.** The degree of ease in which assets can be turned into readily available cash.

**Listed.** Investment securities that have met the listing requirements of a particular exchange.

**Load.** Denotes a mutual fund's initial or deferred sales charge. See also back end load, front end load, and no load.

**Margin.** The capital (in cash or securities) that an investor deposits with a broker to borrow additional funds to purchase securities.

**Margin Call.** A demand from a broker for additional cash or securities as collateral to bring the margin account back within maintenance limits.

**Market Cycle.** A variation in prices that comes full-circle, usually consisting of a decline in excess of 20 percent and a subsequent advance of at least 25 percent.

**Market Risk.** The uncertainty of returns due to fluctuations in the overall market.

**Market Timing.** Measuring the direction of a market or a market index and moving funds in or out of the market based on those measurements. A method of reducing risk exposure to the market. Classic market timing usually involves 100 percent moves between stocks and cash. See also tactical asset allocation.

**Mechanical System.** A trading system that automatically generates buy and sell signals when a set of conditions have been reached.

**Momentum Indicator.** A market indicator using price and volume data to predict strength or weakness and possible turning points.

**Monetary Analysis.** The study of money flows into and out of the economy. Useful in predicting interest rates and market direction.

**Money Markets.** Short-term low-risk investments such as T-Bills, bank CDs, commercial paper, and bankers acceptances.

**Moving Average.** A mathematical procedure used to smooth out fluctuations in data.

**Municipal Bond.** A bond issued by a local or state government or government agency.

**Mutual Fund.** An investment company that sells shares in itself to the investing public and uses the proceeds to purchase individual securities.

**Naked Option.** An option written when the investor does not have a position in the underlying security.

**NASD.** The National Association of Securities Dealers, Inc. The self-regulatory body for the broker/dealer community.

**NASDAQ.** National Association of Securities Dealers Automated Quotation System, providing computerized quotes of market makers for stocks traded over the counter.

**Net Asset Value (NAV).** The quoted market value of a mutual fund share. Determined by dividing the closing market value of all securities owned by the mutual fund plus all other assets and liabilities by the total number of shares outstanding.

**Net Worth.** Assets minus liabilities.

**Neural Network.** An example-based artificial intelligence system that can automatically test and update a knowledge base or set of rules or facts.

**No Load Fund.** A mutual fund sold to the public at net asset value (NAV), with no sales charges.

**Open-End Fund.** Also known as a mutual fund. Distinguished from a closed-end fund by a continuous offering of shares and a commitment to repurchase outstanding shares at net asset value.

**Option.** A security that gives the holder the right to purchase or sell a particular investment at a fixed price for a specified period of time.

**Out Of The Money.** A call option whose striking price is higher than the underlying security's current market price; a put option whose striking price is lower than the current market price.

**Overbought.** Market prices that have risen too far and too fast, overextended.

**Oversold.** Market prices that have declined too far too fast, overextended.

**Policy Asset Allocation.** An asset allocation strategy with a long-term "normal" asset allocation mix.

**Portfolio.** The investment holdings of an individual or institutional investor; including stocks, bonds, options and money market accounts.

**Portfolio Manager.** The individual or individuals responsible for overall investment strategy, as well as, the buying and selling decisions for the securities in the portfolio.

**Price/Earnings Ratio.** Determined by dividing the stock's market price by its earnings per common share. Used as an indicator of company performance and in comparison with other stock investments and the overall market.

**Price-Weighted Index.** A market average such as the Dow Jones Industrial Average that takes into account only the price of each security in the index, thus is unduly influenced by a high priced stock.

**Prime Rate.** The interest rate charged on loans by major banks to their best commercial customers.

**Private Placement.** The placement of a security directly with a person, business, or other entity without any offering to the general investing public.

**Program Trading.** Transactions based on signals from computer programs, usually entered directly from the trader's computer to the market's computer system.

**Prospectus.** The SEC-required printed summary of the registration statement. The prospectus contains critical information about the security offering such as business, management, financial data and risks.

**Put Option.** A contract giving the holder the right to sell the underlying security at a specific price over a specified time frame.

**Qualified Plan.** A retirement plan approved by the I.R.S. and eligible for favorable tax treatment. Earnings on plan assets are not taxed until they are withdrawn or distributed.

**Random Walk.** Investment theory implying that market moves follow no rhyme or reason.

**Range.** The high and low prices over which the security trades during a specific time frame such as day, month and 52-weeks.

**Rating.** Independent ranking of a security in regard to risk and ability to meet payment obligations. Major ratings services include Moodys, Standard & Poors, and Fitch.

**Rebalancing.** The process of adjusting a portfolio mix to return to a desired asset allocation level.

**Registered Investment Advisor.** One who has registered with the SEC to provide investment advice or analysis on securities. Also known as an investment counselor or money manager.

**Relative Strength.** Comparison of a security's price movement in relation to its competitors, its industry, or the entire market.

**Risk.** The financial uncertainty that the actual return will vary from the expected return. Risk factors include inflation, deflation, interest rate risk, market risk, liquidity and default.

**Risk-Adjusted Return.** Presentation of performance results to account for risk incurred to achieve such results. Puts performance comparison on an equivalent-risk basis.

**Risk Management.** An investment strategy designed to reduce the exposure to market risk when the probability of loss is high. See also, active, dynamic, and tactical asset allocation, and market timing.

**SAAFTI.** The Society of Asset Allocators and Fund Timers, Inc.

**Seasonality Trading.** A strategy for effecting trades during seasonally favorable periods such as first of the month and around holidays.

**SEC.** The United States Securities and Exchange Commission. The legislatively-mandated regulatory body for the broker/dealer and investment advisory communities.

**Secondary Market.** Market where previously issued securities trade such as the New York Stock Exchange.

**Sector Fund.** A mutual fund that focuses the majority of its investments in a single industry.

**Security.** An investment that signifies an ownership or creditor position in a corporation.

**SEP-IRA.** A simplified employee pension plan, where contributions are made directly to an employee's IRA account. Much simpler to administer than a 401(k).

**Sharpe Ratio.** A classic risk/return measure, expressed as portfolio return minus risk-free return divided by the portfolio's standard deviation.

**Short Against The Box.** Investment strategy of selling short while holding a long position in the security.

**Short Interest Ratio.** A calculation that indicates the number of trading days required to repurchase all of the shares that have been sold short.

**Short Sale.** Sale of a security not yet owned in order to capitalize on an anticipated market price drop.

**Short Squeeze.** Rapid price rise forcing investors to cover their short positions. This drives the security price up even higher, often squeezing even more short investors.

**Specialist.** A trader on the floor exchange assigned to make a market in a specific stock.

**Split.** A change in the number of outstanding shares through board of directors' action. Shareholder's equity remains the same, each shareholder receives the new stock in proportion to his holdings on the date of record. Dividends and earnings per share are adjusted to reflect the stock split.

**Spread.** In a stock quotation, it's the difference between the bid and ask price. In mergers and acquisitions, it's the difference, either in dollars or as a percentage, between the current market price of the target company's securities and its expected value upon completion of the transaction. In trading, it's a transaction in which two related contracts/stocks/bonds/options are traded to exploit the relative differences in price change between the two.

**S&P 500.** A broad-based stock index composed of 400 industrial, 40 financial, 40 utility, and 20 transportation stocks.

**Standard Deviation.** A measure of the fluctuation in a security's price over time. The lower the standard deviation, theoretically, the less the risk.

**Stock Index Futures.** A futures contract that uses a market index as the underlying instrument.

**Stop Loss.** The risk management technique in which the

security is liquidated to halt any further decline in portfolio value.

**Strategic Asset Allocation.** Very similar strategy to passive asset allocation. Uses principles of modern portfolio theory and the efficient frontier to set dedicated allocation percentages or targets. Rebalancing back to the target is performed periodically to adjust for differences in performance (usually ±5 percent or more).

**Striking Price.** The price at which an option or future contract can be executed according to the terms of the contract. Also called exercise price.

**Style.** See investment style.

**Switching.** Selling one security and purchasing another.

**Synthetic Securities.** Securities created by buying and writing a combination of options that mirror the risk and reward profile of a security.

**Tactical Asset Allocation.** A version of market timing. It can utilize more than just the two asset classes of classic market timing (stock and cash), but employs the same principles of market measurement and risk control in response to changing economic and market conditions. The risk tolerance of the investor is assumed to remain constant.

**10K, 10Q.** Annual and quarterly reports required by the Securities and Exchange Commission. They contain more in-depth financial and operating information than the annual and quarterly stockholder's reports.

**Technical Analysis.** Investment strategy that focuses on market and stock price and volume patterns.

**Top-Down Investing.** Investment strategy starting with

the overall economic scenario and then moving downward to consider industry and individual company investments.

**Total Return.** The return achieved by combining both the dividend/interest and capital appreciation earned on an investment.

**Total Return Index.** A market average such as the NYSE TR Index that gives equal weighting to the daily price changes of every issue in the average.

**Trading Range.** The spread between the high and low prices for a given period of time.

**Treasuries.** United States Government guaranteed securities. Among them, from shortest to longest, are Treasury Bills, Treasury Notes, and Treasury Bonds.

**Trend.** The prevailing tendency or price movement of a set of data as related to time.

**Trend Following.** Moving in the direction of the prevailing price movement.

**Turnaround.** A positive change in the fortunes of a company or industry. Turnarounds occur for a variety of reasons such as economic upturn, new management, new product lines, and strategic acquisitions.

**12b-1.** An annual charge deducted from fund assets to pay for distribution and marketing expenses. Often, after a certain period of time, funds charging a 12b-1 allow shareholders to convert to a class of shares without this fee.

**Ulcer Index.** A measure of price volatility over time that attempts to disregard upside volatility and measure the relative pain of downside volatility.

**Underlying Security.** The security which may be bought or sold under the terms of an option agreement, warrant, etc.

**Undervalued Situation.** A security with a market value that does not fully value its potential or the true value of the company.

**Uptrend.** Upward movement in the market price of a stock.

**Value Averaging.** An investment purchase method that concentrates on the investment's value, not its cost.

**Variable Annuity.** An insurance company contract providing for tax-free buildup of earnings, but whose return is not fixed, but variable, depending on the value of the underlying investments.

**Volatility.** A measure of a security's tendency to move up and down in price. Beta and standard deviation are measures of volatility.

**Volume.** The number of units of a security traded during a given time frame.

**Warrant.** An option to purchase a stated number of shares at a specified price within a specific time frame. Warrants are typically offered as sweeteners to enhance the marketability of stock or debt issues.

**Whipsaw.** Losing money on both sides of a price swing.

**Yield.** An investment's return from its interest or dividend paying capability.

**Yield To Maturity.** The yield of a bond to maturity based on its current market price. The yield to maturity is greater than its stated yield if the bond is selling at a discount from face value and less than its stated yield if the bond is selling at a premium to face value.

**Zero Coupon.** A bond selling at a discount to maturity value and earning interest over the life of the bond but paying no cash dividend until maturity.

# Index

## Symbols

1929  42, 49, 52, 64, 73, 88,
101, 145, 147, 151
1987  41, 140, 143
401(k)  24, 78, 79, 81, 128

## A

Active risk management  17,
19, 26, 37, 41, 46, 47,
48, 53, 54, 60, 61, 64,
68, 69, 74, 87, 90, 93,
97, 98, 99, 100, 103,
121, 122, 130, 152, 153,
154
Alexander, Colin  140
Allocation Plus  148, 149,
151
American Skandia  106
Annuity
Fixed  128, 129
Variable  24, 106, 120,
126, 127, 128, 129, 130,
131, 132, 133, 134, 135,
137, 138
Asset allocation
Dynamic  46, 69, 70, 72,
74, 75, 76, 77
Passive  67, 69, 70, 76,
77, 153
Strategic  70
Tactical  46, 51, 98

## B

Baby boomer  17, 128, 134
Barra/Micropal  75
Bear market  17, 19, 27, 31,
37, 39, 40, 42, 43, 44,
45, 46, 48, 54, 57, 58,
59, 60, 61, 64, 68, 70,
72, 73, 75, 77, 79, 87,
88, 89, 90, 91, 92, 94,
99, 100, 101, 102, 103,
104, 121, 141, 142, 143,
144, 145, 146, 151, 152,
153
Belsky, Gary  78, 120
Bogle, John C.  37, 47, 51
Bonds  23, 24, 35, 37, 50,
51, 67, 68, 69, 76, 89,
105
Brown, John Dennis  45
Budget  22
Buffett, Warren  47, 48, 49,

53, 147

Bull market  17, 19, 41, 45,
   58, 64, 70, 79, 87, 88,
   91, 92, 102, 104, 121,
   128, 145, 146

Buy and hold  17, 37, 39,
   40, 41, 42, 43, 44, 46,
   47, 48, 49, 52, 54, 56,
   58, 59, 61, 64, 67, 76,
   84, 85, 88, 89, 91, 92,
   93, 94, 96, 99, 100, 101,
   102, 103, 152, 153

**C**

Cabot, Paul C.  52
Carver, Bob  88
Case, Karl  30
Cassidy, Donald L.  53
Certificates of deposit  23,
   35, 98
Chance, Don  98
Closet market timers  47, 52
Colby, Robert W.  101
Collectibles  18, 32, 33, 34
Common stocks  37, 48
Compound interest  23, 26,
   135
Compounding  23
Computer simulations  46,
   98, 100, 105, 149
Cost of living  24

**D**

Danko, William D.  24
DeForest, Lee  96
Depression  31, 35
Diamonds  33
Discipline  19, 26, 40, 41,
   99, 109
Diversification  57, 67, 75,
   78, 80, 81, 82

Dividend yield  50
Dobbs, Lou  103
Dollar cost averaging  52,
   58, 59, 60, 61, 134, 152
Donoghue, William E.  36,
   75
Dow (Dow Jones Industrials)
   42, 48, 49, 86, 101, 140,
   145
Drawdown  19, 101, 106,
   151

**E**

Economist, The  28, 29
Efficient Market Theory  62,
   63
Emotional  25, 40, 41, 46,
   53, 54, 68, 76, 98, 102,
   152
Evensky, Harold  28, 30
Evergreen S4 (small compa-
   nies) Fund  44
Evolution  70, 71

**F**

Farmer, Doyne  66
Farrell, Robert  99
Federal Reserve  142
Fidelity  47, 63
  Magellan  44, 50, 51, 75
Fixed income  36, 37, 68
Flexible Plan  70, 71, 106,
   148, 151
Forbes, Malcolm S., Jr.  49
Fosback, Norman G.  62
Franklin, Ben  21
Freeburg, Nelson  74

**G**

Gilovich, Thomas  78, 120

Gipson, Jim  144
Goals  112, 120, 134, 151
Graham, Benjamin  48, 49,
     147, 151

**H**

Hartle, Thom  114
Hemler, Michael  98
Huggard, John P.  133
Hulbert, Mark  123, 124

**I**

Ideal investment  45, 46, 54
Income  19, 21, 22, 23, 24,
     25, 27, 28, 29, 30, 31,
     33, 34, 79, 90, 107, 108,
     130, 132, 137, 138
Indicators  62, 74, 99, 120,
     147
Inflation  24, 25, 26, 28, 29,
     33, 35, 36, 37, 40, 45,
     50, 54, 59, 72, 90, 98,
     102, 142, 143, 152
Insana, Ron  63
Interest rate  29, 36, 51, 128
Inverse fund  104, 105, 107
Investment advisor  26, 27,
     30, 55, 65, 74, 103, 110,
     111, 112, 118, 119, 123
IRS Code Section 1035  130
Israelsen, Craig  56

**J**

John Hancock  138

**K**

Kelley, Fred  108
Kiely, Dr. Joe  63
Kilpatrick, Andrew  48
Kurtz, Howard  113

**L**

Lardner, Dionysius  96
Lefevre, Edwin  140
Liquidity  30, 31, 46, 55,
     127
Livermore, Jesse  112, 121
Lo, Andrew W.  63
Loeper, David B.  69
Lopes, Lola  91
Lynch, Peter  47, 50, 63, 64

**M**

Mackey, Mark J.  127
MacKinlay, A. Craig  63
Market cycle  45, 72, 87,
     120, 125, 145
Market timing  46, 47, 48,
     49, 50, 51, 52, 53, 64,
     74, 83, 87, 88, 91, 93,
     94, 95, 96, 98, 100, 130
Markowitz, Harry  69
Merrill, Peter  127
Merriman, Paul  36, 41, 91
Meyers, Thomas A.  101
Money  29
Money market  35, 98, 104,
     105, 106
Moving average  64
Murray, Nick  35
Mutual fund  22, 23, 24, 39,
     41, 42, 51, 52, 54, 55,
     56, 57, 81, 89, 91, 104,
     107, 108, 109, 120, 122,
     126, 127, 128, 129, 130,
     133, 134, 135, 137

**N**

NASDAQ  40, 65, 102, 105,
     106, 107, 144, 145
National Association for

Variable Annuities (NAVA)  127
Nationwide Marketflex  106
Net worth  22, 23, 24, 107, 108
NYSE TR Index  44

**O**

Oppenheimer, Joseph L.  76

**P**

Paine Webber  143
Patience (in investing)  19, 120
Paul, Rich  53, 98
Peters, Edgar  62
Prechter, Robert R., Jr.  30, 45, 105
Price/earnings ratio  29, 143
ProFunds  105, 106, 138
Prudential  138
Purchasing power  24, 35

**R**

Random Walk  62, 63, 64, 66
Real estate  22, 29, 30, 31
Real wealth  21, 22, 23
Reinhart, Len  117
Retirement  17, 18, 21, 23, 25, 26, 30, 31, 33, 36, 40, 41, 59, 60, 72, 78, 80, 89, 90, 109, 127, 128, 129, 130, 131, 132, 134, 138, 152
Rich  21, 23, 24, 27, 28, 29, 30, 33, 34, 80
Risk  25, 26, 29, 35, 36, 37, 38, 43, 46, 51, 53, 54, 55, 58, 60, 61, 64, 67, 68, 69, 72, 75, 77, 78, 79, 82, 89, 90, 91, 97, 98, 99, 101, 104, 107, 111, 117, 120, 129, 134, 139, 144, 146, 148, 149, 151, 153, 154
Risk management  17, 19, 54, 83, 87, 91, 92, 94, 105, 114, 138, 144, 154
Risk-adjusted returns  26, 53, 64, 66, 72, 76, 77, 87, 96, 97, 98, 99, 153
Rydex  105, 106

**S**

S&P 500  40, 50, 65, 79, 80, 85, 89, 101, 102, 104, 105, 107, 142, 145, 147
SAAFTI  26, 27, 53
Samuelson, Paul  40
Schreiner, Roger  65, 148
Sector funds  47
Security Benefit  106
Select Advisors  65, 148
Shaffner, George  21
Sharpe, Bill  69
Shellans, Steve  98, 116
Sheperdson, James, III  127
Shiller, Robert J.  109
Shilling, A. Gary  141
Siegel, Jeremy J.  37, 64
SIMCO  61, 71, 93, 97, 106
Smith, Adam  77
Smithers, Andrew  55, 56
Stack, James B.  147
Stanley, Thomas J.  24
Stewart, Martha  118
Stock fund  90, 105, 107, 133
Systematic withdrawal  89, 132

# T

T-Bills  35, 36, 98
Tax-deferred  23, 24, 46,
     107, 126, 128, 129, 131,
     135, 137
Templeton, Sir John  39, 51,
     104, 146
Thomson, William  95

# V

VARDS Report  128
Variable annuities.  *See* See
     Annuity, Variable
Variable universal life  137,
     138, 139
Volatility  107, 116

# W

Wagner, Jerry  70, 73, 98,
     148
Warner, Harry M.  95
Wells, Bruce F.  126
White, Jerry  67
Worth  51
Wright, Stephen  55, 56

# Y

Yield  50, 131

# Z

Zandi, Mark  30
Zweig, Marty  83

Printed in the United States
38727LVS00002B/84